Steve

THE TROJAN HORSE

To my daughters, Nora and Alma

Göran Adamson

THE TROJAN HORSE

A Leftist Critique of Multiculturalism in the West

ISBN: 978-91-639-5142-8

Content

Preface to the English edition 6

Preface by Per Bauhn 7

Preface by Jens-Martin Eriksen 10

Author's preface 11

1 Multiculturalism in the West 13

2 Sweden – The epicentre of multiculturalism 22

3 The story of a Social Democratic mantra 30

4 On ethnic reflection and how to gain public recognition 53

5 Internationalisation and neoliberalism 67

6 Diversity or racism – is it that simple? 84

7 Pedestals, populism and pseudo radicalism 100

8 Diversity plans at eight universities 124

9 How is the ideology of diversity being legitimised? 135

10 Six cases of criticism 148

11 Autonomy or compliance – how did the universities respond? 159

Notes 166

List of References 177

Preface to the English edition

Nov. 13, 2015, was the French 9/11. On that day, 130 people were shot dead in a series of coordinated attacks in Paris – the epicentre of the Enlightenment. In Bataclan alone, where people were listening to live music and having fun, 89 lost their lives. 368 were injured. On that day, modern society came under attack.

Difference, they say, is worth fighting for. It goes under the name of multiculturalism. In Paris, this idea failed. At the end of the multicultural road of difference, we do not find excitement, fascination or anything of the sort, but – at best – indifference, if not distrust, misunderstanding, confusion, hostility and hate.

The murders in Paris did not occur despite multiculturalism, but was a direct result of it. When a marriage is characterized by those multicultural virtues – distance, lack of shared views, confusion of tongues etc. divorce is imminent. Diversity and multiculturalism is a danger for society as we know it. Paris is but another case in point.

I was late to the meeting of Fri Debat, at Information, the Copenhagen quality newspaper. I managed to gain the attention of the camera man inside, who unlocked the door.

I could not make it to the following meeting at Krudtönden. Finn Nörgaard, who had opened the door for me, tried to dissuade the Islamist from shooting and was gunned down.

Some 40 000 people attended the manifestation. Speakers talked about inter-faith dialogue. Sadly, there was not a headscarf in sight. Then we listened to John Lennon's Imagine: 'Nothing to kill or die for, and no religion too'. Lennon was a classic leftist: sexually liberated, provocative and deeply anti-religious.

The old left and the new, multicultural left is separated by nothing short of an abyss.

Göran Adamson
Ph.D
September 2017

Preface by Per Bauhn

The late 18th century revolutions reshaped the West and lay the foundation for democracy, as we know it. In this process, reason, freedom, and equality were key words. Those who in the early days opposed these values are generally referred to as belonging to the political right and to the conservative camp. They sought to defend King, Church, tradition, nation as a historical entity, and rights based upon ancestry and class. The political left, liberals and socialists aspired, in contrast, to universal suffrage and the abolition of estates and guilds, defending enlightenment and rationality.

Today the political map is less straightforward. The political right no longer refers to tradition and nation, but rather to what is in the interest of transformation and global capitalism. At the same time, the political left, along with parts of the liberal centre, has drifted from an individually based ideal of equal opportunities towards an ideal based on structural justice, i.e. equality of outcome between groups. (For instance, it may concern women as opposed to men, or ethnic minorities in relation to the majority population.) In recent years, Sweden has been dominated by the ideal of structural justice. The explicit ambition, at this point, is to foster diversity in the sense that 'marginalised' groups ought to be represented in education and work, not the least in leading positions, in proportion to the percentage of the population.

The old left, fighting for universal suffrage, never demanded that the number of workers in the parliament should be proportionate to their percentage in society. All they insisted upon was universal suffrage. To the old left, access to higher education should be open to any qualified candidate irrespective of economic background. It never insisted that a certain proportion of university students should be working-class.

As a result of the model of structural justice, group identity is seen as of greater importance than individual choice. As a result of the ideology of diversity, criticising minority groups already perceived as vulnerable is seen as improper. Discussions about honour crime and artistic challenges against taboos in Islam are good cases in point. As a result of an idealisation of vulnerable groups, the wider community has abandoned dissenting individuals within these groups. No matter how vital values such as reason and freedom may be for democracy and civil rights, we tend to shy away from them, the moment they clash with the norm systems of these minority groups.

As clearly pointed out by Göran Adamson, the concept of diversity is in dire need of a more thorough investigation. Is diversity necessarily a good thing? It depends. (Is polygamy better than monogamy?) When the ideology of diversity is being championed based on certain distinct identities, the result is as arbitrary as the discrimination one is set to oppose in the first place.

The universities are at the core of Adamson's book. How do they serve democracy? Not, the author argues, by thinking the way politicians want them to think. Instead, one should think without inhibitions in order to be able to express ideas that might never have surfaced otherwise, not by politicians nor by their constituencies. Reason and freedom, core democratic values, are also crucial to the university.

When the institution of the university is requested to affirm the value of diversity in the 'recruitment' of students, its role as an arena of free debate, Adamson points out, is being challenged. No matter how well intentioned any political decrees may be, they can never be exempt from critical thinking. Worth adding, universities do not 'recruit' students. Universities offer educations and students *apply* for them. Only if students are being recruited can we talk about discrimination, and the rhetoric of exclusion requires, in turn, discrimination. (In a similar fashion, work applicants who are not selected are described as 'excluded', which gives an image of bad intentions and hence culpability.)

In addition, one may, as Adamson does, ask: Why do Swedish universities so submissively accept the ideology of diversity and present diversity plans to show it? They get money from politicians, so they need good relations to politicians. In addition, probably, they dislike the idea of conflict. Swimming against the tide is seen as disloyal and as an obstruction. Your own views are subordinate to what you are supposed to think. It is easier to err together than to draw the right conclusions on your own. Not much has happened since old times and their crooked suspicion against dissenting views. We talk about diversity, but we are not even close to individual independence. The situation at the university is no exception.

Per Bauhn
Professor, Practical Philosophy,
The University of Linné

Preface by Jens-Martin Eriksen

It is widely known that various themes in the process of time may shift from one political extreme to another. Once upon a time, protection of nature was important to conservatives, and then the left adopted it. The idea of culture is no different. Previously, the European right exclusively proclaimed it. Today the left has taken up this ideology – but it is nonetheless a reactionary ideology. In the case of Sweden, Göran Adamson clearly shows how the left has let a Trojan horse over the threshold. His ambition can be compared to the French journalist and author, Caroline Fourest, and her book *La tentation obscurantiste*, and the ways in which the once Universalist left turned (multi)culturalist. His book is about a European phenomenon, leading to a fatal crisis. The way Göran Adamson's book in Sweden will be received will be part of this crisis. Either, as true progressives, commentators will embrace a critique against a progressive project in utter disarray. Or are the hegemonic culturist dogmas still untouchable?

Jens-Martin Eriksen
Co-author of *The Democratic Contradictions of Multiculturalism*

Author's preface

Multiculturalism is a conservative idea, which is seen as progressive. Multiculturalism and diversity are about background, ethnicity, belonging, spokespersons and roots. Those who talk about roots talk about an idyll of the past, a historical Eldorado in contrast to universal suffrage, technological progress, and everything else that belongs to modern society. A conservative ideology does not become more radical just because it is being cherished by journalists, politicians, and academics who say they are.

Critiques against diversity, we are told, come from the right. This book takes the opposite position. Convincing criticism against diversity always comes from a leftist perspective, from those who advocate meritocracy instead of group rights, majority and democracy instead of adoration of minorities, equality between men and women instead of patriarchy, the rule of law instead of 'minority legislation', science instead of belief, debate instead of censorship, modernity and the bliss of forgetting instead of an obsession with historical injustice. The only Swedish political party talking about roots with enthusiasm similar to that of advocates of diversity, is Sverigedemokraterna, (Sweden Democrats) a right-wing populist party. Moreover, the ideology of diversity shows numerous similarities with neoliberalism. Neoliberalism profits from diversity, and diversity comes in handy to the neoliberals. The Swedish establishment has allowed a Trojan horse into it's midst.

Göran Adamson
Hanoi 2017-02-12

Multiculturalism in the West

Mister West! How nice of you to join us tonight and add colour to these monochromatic proceedings!

Dr Arliss Loveless in *Wild, Wild West*[1]

This book endeavours to assess the general ideology of multiculturalism critically. A few key questions will be discussed:

- Multiculturalists have replaced class with culture. What are the consequences?
- Racists single out immigrants for criticism. Multiculturalists single out immigrants to be idealised. What is the difference, really?
- Multiculturalism claims to be an anti-elitist project. Why, then, are domestic working-class people and working-class people from overseas baited against each other?
- Diversity and 'being different' fuels, it is claimed, understanding. Well, does it?
- What happens to us as individuals under that majestic edifice of multiculturalism?
- Ethnicity is good, we are told, and nationalism is bad. Why?
- Multiculturalism is portrayed as progressive and radical. Is that so?

These questions and others will be dealt with by means of a case study – Sweden. For anyone seeking the ideology of multiculturalism at its deepest and most all pervasive, no country offers a better example than Sweden. An institution was chosen where the study of multiculturalism should be as free from political surveillance as possible – the university. If independent discussions about multiculturalism existed at all, the university should be the place for it.

In order to put the Swedish discussion in context, the book will commence with a brief overview of the international discussion on multiculturalism. The purpose is to show that the ideology of multiculturalism is a strong undercurrent throughout the developed world. A few countries have been singled out. The discussion will be conducted by theme, and the themes touched upon will reoccur throughout the book.

In a November 2013 issue of *the New York Times*, the headline read: 'Does TV Capture the Diversity of America Yet'?[2] The question is a poignant expression of a particular attitude towards – among other things – entertainment. What are the criteria by which participants on TV should be categorised? Is it by means of individual qualifications? Or should it rather be dealt with via 'representation', 'mirroring', or 'reflection' of one's own ethnic, religious, and cultural group? The arguments seem to weigh heavily on the side of multicultural representation and, in case we shift to the United Kingdom, the British BBC expresses similar views. The BBC aims, as announced by their *Diversity Plan*, 'to reflect the diversity of the UK and make our services accessible to all'. Hence, TV-programs are made accessible to ethnic minority groups through representation – because other co-members of their group are shown on TV. The TV programs have to reflect 'Britain accurately and authentically'. For instance, critics were dismayed by the fact that the TV-show *East Enders*, was almost 'twice as white' as the real East End.[3]

One should note here a connection to the interest of business. When institutions seek to adhere to ethnic quotas and to mirror surrounding society, they also claim to protect 'their image'. The French EU-site entitled *Chartre de la Diversité en Enterprise* (Diversity Charter in Enterprise) brings up the question why businesses and society should 'make a commitment' in favour of diversity. Because 'It is a win-win situation'. It provides 'social cohesiveness', and offers 'protection from damage to their reputation'. 'Striving for diversity', then, means 'building a positive corporate image'. If we foster diversity we are 'socially responsible'.[4] At SALTO YOUTH – an ambitious EU network working on 'European priority areas' – 'the business case for diversity' is advocated for.[5] Increasing diversity will improve knowledge about how to operate in different cultures, widen 'the talent base' and enhance the company's 'image'.[6] 'Over the long term', the French Diversity Charter continues, 'a diversity team' brings a whole range of positive effects: it 'provides a better understanding of the needs of different customer bases, helps penetrate new markets, develop the company's capacity for innovation and gives greater flexibility during times of change'.[7]

As noted above, the benefits of diversity are often taken for granted. Therefore, we shall now give examples of the intimate link between diversity and quality, and its repercussions. As claimed by Mark Thompson, Director General of the BBC, 'In case the BBC is to successfully deliver *Putting Quality First*', it must, 'in programmes' and 'in the stories we tell, as well as through the people we work with', showcase 'the UK's complexity and diversity – on and off air'. And quality, he continues, brings originality because quality 'is a creative opportunity' in case we wish to tell 'new and original stories'. Quality allows for 'genuinely distinctive content'.[8] The ideology of diversity is therefore seen as vital in order to avoid bland and unassuming entertainment. Quality and originality require individuals from overseas. As an example of a spin-off effect of this assumed link between diversity and quality, Malta recently launched its first newspaper 'dedicated to the promotion of cultural diversity'.[9] Turning from Malta to Germany, a site titled 'Umgang mit Migrantinnen und Migranten' (Interaction with Migrants) under *Bundeszentrale für Politische Bildung*, claims that diversity and multiculturalism do more good than harm, and that Germany, as a consequence, is 'enriched' by it.[10] In 2014, the British Royal Air Force was given the title of 'Diversity Champion of the Year' by EDA – European Diversity Awards – an EU-linked organisation that 'recognises and celebrates those organisations and individuals that have shown innovation, creativity and commitment to equality, diversity and inclusion'! The EDA awards are, as claimed on the webpage, 'widely acknowledged as the "Oscars of diversity"'.[11] The case 'for exploring diversity is simple.'[12]

If diversity is tantamount to quality, the task on the part of its adherents is not ideological but merely educational. Diversity becomes a question of information. Pedagogic phrases such as 'tools' and 'training' are common. The EU-funded project entitled *Approach to*

Cultural Diversity in Italy is 'aimed at providing companies the necessary knowledge and tools to manage the cultural diversity'. Focus on information means that those who fail to embrace diversity are uninformed. The EU-youth project above insists that diversity is promoted – and racism tackled – by means of 'awareness raising and education'.[13] In Spain, teachers are to be subject to 'training in cultural diversity',[14] and diversity will 'help people recognise, understand and challenge attitudes and behaviour'.[15] To overcome racism effectively, only multicultural 'awareness raising, education, and opening of the spirit by getting to know others', as claimed by Yéra Dembélé, Director at the Liaison Euro-Africaine, 'can have a sustainable effect'. The underlying idea is that all conflicts are caused by insufficient contact – i.e. lack of information about people from other cultural backgrounds.[16]

As shown above, the ideology of diversity in the West is characterised by the need for ethnic representation, a belief that diversity is inherently good and, hence, that information – not arguments – are required. Another attitude that pervades multiculturalism throughout the West has to do with a desire to associate it with well-reputed views and ideas.

Next to Sweden, Britain stands out as a special case regarding diversity, and the BBC is again a useful example. As claimed by its diversity plan, the BBC 'is committed to promoting equal opportunities for all'.[17] More common, however, is to attach diversity to a particularly esteemed political concept – the notion of equality. *The Polish Diversity Charter* – the country's charter of a European Commission diversity initiative – is a good case in point. This charter is 'aimed at encouraging companies to implement and develop diversity policies'.[18] The charter promotes 'equal treatment' as well as human rights. In a similar initiative, the EU's 'Guide to European Diversity' underscored that '"United in diversity" is an underlying principle of the European Union'.[19] The first country where multiculturalism was established on a grand scale was Canada in 1971. 'Canadian Multiculturalism', a Canadian government website announces, 'is fundamental to our belief that all citizens are equal'. Multiculturalism and the idea of citizenship are, therefore, fused.

The excerpt continues: 'Multiculturalism ensures that all citizens can keep their identities, can take pride in their ancestry and have a sense of belonging', and ends: 'The Canadian experience has shown that multiculturalism encourages racial and ethnic harmony and cross-cultural understanding'.[20] The statement assumes that proximity between cultures also brings them closer together in terms of shared views.

Similarly to equal opportunities and equality, individualism has strong positive connotations. British State Television provides the following message: 'We value and respect every individual's unique contribution (…) and seek to ensure that no one group or individual is unlawfully disadvantaged'. Group rights are, consequently, combined with individual rights, and collectivism, by implication, with individualism. Still, the individual is only present on occasion. The diversity plan of the BBC starts out by observing that there 'are around 60 million people in the UK', and continues: 'we are all different by virtue of our own particular circumstances: from age and gender, disability and race, religion and sexual orientation, where we come from and where we choose to be – and other circumstances that form who we are and what our story is'.[21] Individual differences or dissenting views against the grain of the group are missing. The 'story' is never mine, but ours. In a similar vein, 'dialogues' – habitually brought forth in diversity rhetoric, are always between 'cultures', and non-European lands are labelled 'alien'. A book cherishing diversity in Germany wonders to what extent European television 'thematizes alien cultures', and suggests that we must 'recognize the opportunities of cultural dialogues'.[22] This is a faceless conversation between cultures. Is the individual autonomous or anonymous?

Finally, there are plenty of cases where diversity is combined with internationalisation. The meaning of the concept below is close to globalisation, as in 'international exchange of students'. In the EU-funded 'Approach to cultural diversity in Italy', it is argued that immigrants 'within companies can help the enterprise establish new international relationships'.[23] But it is not clear why an individual would open up an organisation to international trade relations just because he or she is from overseas. Your passport, for instance, says nothing about your education.

Above, it was noted that the case for diversity and multiculturalism is merely educational. The sceptics must not, in other words, be convinced but solely informed. About what? About the benefits of sharing common space. 'Multicultural' implies, precisely, that we are better off living together, albeit separated by the borders of ethnicity, culture, race, skin colour, and so on. Understanding brings us together, and conflicts arise because our thoughts are confused. These ideas were clearly expressed by the Suffolk County Council community spokesperson in 2005: 'Intolerance towards others', he maintained, 'is often more from a lack of knowledge than hatred or spite. And therefore, the more we know about each other and our neighbours, the greater chance we have of understanding and appreciating the differences between us'.[24]

The flagship of diversity, however, goes under the name of 'anti-racism'. Diversity prevents racism, and racism obstructs multiculturalism. Britain, it is publically announced, is 'committed to providing a working environment that is free from harassment, intimidation and unlawful discrimination'.[25] Assigning special attention to diversity and to ethnic minority groups best fights racism. According to the *Maltese Organization for Friendship in Diversity*, the 'simplest (...) way to combat racist stereotypes and xenophobic attitudes at their roots' is to 'promote friendship through diversity'.[26] Communication infused by the ideology of multiculturalism is seen as an anti-racist endeavour. When protagonists of diversity embrace ethnic minorities, it often comes in the form of festivals and performances. A good example is the multicultural Notting Hill Carnival in London, going back to a Trinidadian tradition and the abolition of slavery in the 1830s. Among diversity's critics, the 2004 French law banning the wearing of overt religious symbols in public schools was seen as beneficial for integration and national solidarity. This law, however, prohibited the wearing of Muslim headscarves. Therefore, diversity's supporters saw the law as profoundly racist – violating religious freedom while fuelling anti-Arab stereotypes.[27]

Among institutions with a strong multicultural influence such as the European Commission, discrimination is fought by diversity. Racism and xenophobia are countered by recognition of 'otherness' and being different. In 2009, one of the EU's 'award-winning articles' was 'about gay football players in a tie with a Danish article about women who convert to Islam'.[28] From this perspective, recognition of commonalities, things we share and political concepts such as citizenship, do not qualify as anti-racist.

Above, I touched upon how important it is for institutions to seek a workforce that accurately reflects its surrounding society. Apart from an alleged quality aspect, another reason was anti-racism, because a diversified staff would hopefully pre-empt 'the risk of discrimination complaints or losing their reputation to legal proceedings'.[29] Diversity, consequently, is an anti-racist endeavour because it fends off allegations of racist and discriminatory hiring practises.

In the eyes of multiculturalists, the nation, the nation state, and nationalism are seen as politically suspicious. The path seamlessly runs from these ideas, via exclusion and segregation, towards racism and fascism. In a 2010 article 'Spain implements a practical approach to managing diversity!', Ricard Zapata-Barrero, writing for the *Council of Europe,* maintains that 'national legal or institutional aspects act like a wall. They block every attempt to bring about innovation and change to the country's diversity management policies'.[30] National law is not about safeguarding and protecting certain principles and thereby allowing for swift and just legal, political, and other proceedings. National law and national institutions stifle innovation and change.

The anti-racism of diversity does not, however, mean that racial categories are absent in diversity rhetoric. They often occur, but as opposed to old-school racism, racial categories are now used to identify and give support to ethnic minority groups. The BBC is committed 'to serve all our audiences'. In order to reach this objective, the BBC is determined 'to visibly increase our diversity on and off air'.[31] Diversity is not, then, about intellectual pluralism, but merely about the visual presence of individuals from overseas.

A related issue has to do with the question of ethnicity compared with class. Throughout the West, the multicultural left has assigned tremendous importance to vertical, ethnic divisions. When ethnicity is being treated as a primary category of identification, horizontal class divisions are obscured. This scheme has enabled the construction of clear-cut borders between natives and immigrants. In 2008, under the title 'Italy gives cultural diversity a lukewarm embrace', *New York Times* had a picture showing local southern Italian residents shouting slogans as a Roma camp burned for the second time in a day in a suburb of Naples.[32] The purpose of the article was to set local domestic, well-off Italians against poor and destitute Roma. But a closer look at the supposedly racist southern Italians in the picture – every second tooth missing and clothes and posture to match – suggests that they were working class at best. In fact, they could have been Roma. Instead of bearing witness to a racist event, the picture suggested a clash within the working class.

Below, the outline of the book will be presented. Then, I shall turn to Sweden – the epicentre of multiculturalism.

The discussion has two key sections. The first is constituted by a critical analysis of *Diversity at the University,* the 260-page Social Democratic report that was to have a huge impact in Sweden. The second section critically examines the diversity plans – one of the consequences of this report. Diversity plans at the eight largest universities have been selected: Stockholm University, Göteborg University, Uppsala University, Lund University, Umeå University, the University of Linné, in Växjö, Linköping University, and Malmö University College. The analysis of Swedish universities represents a case study, demonstrating how multiculturalism has become a hegemonic idea in the West.

The discussion on *Diversity at the University* is divided into five chapters. Chapter 2. 'Sweden – the epicentre of multiculturalism' introduces its particular features in my home country. It also presents a distinction between a right wing critique and a liberal or left wing critique against multiculturalism. Chapter 3. 'The story of a Social Democratic mantra' analyses how diversity is being defined in *Diversity at the University.* Subsequently, the association between diversity and quality is being scrutinised. This link is further investigated in chapter 4., 'On ethnic reflection and how to gain public recognition'. Chapter 5., 'Internationalisation and neoliberalism', shows how the report tries to draw parallels between diversity and internationalisation, while, simultaneously, overlooking links to neoliberalism. A central aspect of the ideology of diversity is brought to the forefront in chapter 6, 'Diversity or racism – is it that simple?' In Chapter 7, 'Pedestals, populism and pseudo radicalism', concludes the discussion about *Diversity at the University.* The task at stake is to examine how diversity tends to overlook the individual in the analysis, polarise the political debate, and trivialise scientific discussion. Then, in chapter 8, 'Diversity plans at eight universities', the topic is shifted to these ideological plans. In chapter 9, 'How is the ideology of diversity being legitimised?' the question is asked whether diversity is 'self-evident', and also if it rests on the authority of natural sciences. Subsequently, it is asked whether diversity is a mere case of information, and if diversity and internationalisation are closely associated. In conclusion, two questions are raised: What is the relation between diversity and social engineering? and, importantly: What is the difference between culturalism of the left (diversity), and culturalism of the right (right-wing populism)?[33] Chapter 10, 'Six cases of criticism' brings to attention whether these diversity plans seek to unite collectivism and individualism, and whether or not their definition of diversity stands the test of empirical analysis. Diversity's rhetoric of difference is problematized, in particular when applied to the realm of the economy. The ideology of diversity cherishes representation by means of ethnic presence instead of ideas. What does this imply? Finally, it is noted that, in Sweden, the vital international discussion is largely absent. Chapter 11, 'Autonomy or compliance – how did the universities respond?' addresses the independence of higher education in relation to official political power. Finally, we turn back to the university as a case study. What does diversity's role in the university tell us about Swedish society, and by implication, about the West?

Sweden – the epicentre of multiculturalism

In late 1999, the then-Social Democratic government commissioned all Swedish public bodies to introduce 'diversity plans' in order to strengthen ethnic diversity among the employed. The bodies responded with great enthusiasm. According to a mapping by the Swedish Agency for Public Management, by 2004, two out of three state bodies had composed a diversity plan.[34] Today, multiculturalism and diversity are integrated in the daily activities of public bodies. On its website, under the heading of 'Equal rights to all', the National Agency for Education mentions 'diversity and equality', and discusses 'the different faces of racism'. 'Racism', it is claimed, 'exists when one ethnic group /.../ dominates over, excludes or strives to exterminate another group'.[35] Under 'Ethnic and cultural diversity', the Swedish Arts Council is commissioned to foster a diversity perspective, which is to be reflected in its entire activities as well as in all aid.[36] The Swedish Board of Agriculture's website supports 'Innovation through diversity when new Swedes meet the countryside'.[37] At the Police Authority in Stockholm County, diversity means that 'the equal value of all human beings should be respected and that all human beings should be judged according to these principles regardless of background and individual discrepancies'.[38] Among other things, the Swedish Church presents: 'Holy dances cherishing diversity, justice and sustainability'.[39] 'Within the frames of its competence supply', it is stated by *Swedish Accident Investigation Authority* from 2008, 'the organization fosters diversity'.[40] Under the heading, "Integration and diversity", the Swedish Government supports, 'a common value foundation in a society characterised by increasing diversity.'[41]

The influence of diversity is as strong in party politics. Entering 'Vänsterpartiet' (Left Party) plus 'diversity' gets 330,000 hits on the net.[42] Accompanying a photo of a few election campaigners – one of them with a foreign background, Miljöpartiet (The Green Party) in Eskilstuna announces: 'We have lovely diversity'.[43] Centerpartiet (Centre Party) supports diversity on the platform called Diversity Group: 'Diversity – provides added value and profit'.[44] Recently, the party has advocated cultural diversity and tolerance by defending, among other things, polygamy. 'Diversity enriches', argues Kristdemokraterna (Christian Democrats).[45] 'Liberal diversity', a society within the Swedish People's Party, insists that 'all politics on all levels must be saturated by diversity',[46] and Moderaterna (the Conservatives) seek to connect the concept to economic development through the expression: 'Diversity – factor for success for a sustainable growth'.[47] The ideology of diversity has never been more successful than within Social Democracy.[48] Today it is more accepted to talk about ethnicity and diversity than about class – which means that the basis of categorisation characterising the left ever since Marx has been abandoned. Majority has been substituted for minority, and politics for culture. The one dissenting party is Sverigedemokraterna (Sweden Democrats). On their homepage under the heading, 'Sweden is in need of a new immigration policy', the party declares: 'We oppose a multicultural society'.[49] This picture is supported in the media. On television, on radio, and in newspapers, the attitude to diversity is overwhelmingly positive.

Consequently, mainstream discourse is strongly characterised by diversity. But, then, what is it really? What are the ideological foundations behind it? Is it true that diversity as a coherent ideology leads to a better and more open-minded society? Or does it rather pave the way for something different?

In order to suggest an answer I have analysed the role of diversity at Swedish universities. This is a case study of a Western phenomenon. In case a critical debate around the notion of diversity exists at all, it does not take place in the press or in party politics. It goes on within the university. 'The university', writes Lennart Lundquist, 'should be a *best case* of freedom of expression, i.e. unless freedom of expression exists at the university, where truth is essential, it most certainly does not exist anywhere'.[50] The role of diversity within the university is a litmus test of society's resistance against ideological dominance.

Below I shall describe the university material chosen to investigate the role of diversity in higher education, and why I have chosen this material. First, however, it is vital to make a scientific distinction between two forms of critique of diversity. This is because diversity is a highly contested topic, often resulting in a polarised and emotional discussion. The distinction below separates rightist critique from leftist critique. This division, it must be acknowledged, is a conscious simplification in order to clarify a conflict. In reality, certainly, the situation is not that simple. As an example, Peter Wood's *Diversity – The Invention of a Concept* relies on a conservative foundation. In concrete terms, however, his discussion falls well within the frames of a democratic leftist tradition.[51]

Starting with the rightist scene, the conservative discussion is most important. A few influential names should be mentioned. In the eyes of Melanie Phillips, British multiculturalism has long since been plagued by irrationalism and apathy. Her discussion is often underpinned by vengeful emotions and moralism.[52] Multiculturalism, Roger Scruton claims, leads to ethno-mysticism. At the same time, he argues, the foundation of the democratic institutions in the West was constituted by religious traditions *predating* the Enlightenment. His criticism against diversity does not presuppose a defence of the Enlightenment. The idea of diversity is – in contrast – perceived as a facet of a progressive ideological framework.[53] Christopher Caldwell's *Reflections on the Revolution in Europe: Immigration, Islam and the West* questions 'liberal tolerance' and thereby suggests that diversity is compatible with liberal views.[54] In *America Alone: The End of the World As We Know it*, Mark Steyn analyses how receding religiosity also tends to result in a demographic downturn.[55] Similar to Phillips, Steyn makes use of forceful collectivist images, and refers, among other things, to Islam as one homogeneous entity.

In Sweden, this conservative critique is largely overlooked. Instead, a more radical rightist critique is being emphasised. It may be racist, fascist, or Nazi and it may be referred to as islamophobic or xenophobic. Above all, this kind of criticism can be found on the Internet. 'Nationell.nu' (National.now) attacks diversity by means of classic sociobiological rhetoric, employing analogies with nature in order to justify the use of political violence.[56] The underlying idea is that diversity is a leftist concept leading to equality and a welfare state, while a rightist favours inequality. 'Nordfront.se' argues along similar lines.[57] Svenska Motståndsrörelsen, making headlines in December 2013 by attacking an anti-racist demonstration in Kärrtorp, belongs to the same group. Under the heading: 'Dismantle the culture of diversity', Nationaldemokraterna (National Democrats) claims that 'others' can live in Sweden only 'as long as it will not jeopardise the survival of the Swedish people as a distinct ethnic group'.[58] Hence, the party argues that ethnicity has a genetic foundation, a view commonly held in fascism and national socialism. The Swedish Defence League (SDL) is linked both with Swedish national socialism and with Bandidos – a criminal motorcycle gang, making use of black-and-white images of minority groups, Muslims in particular. Critiques against diversity by Sverigedemokraterna (Sweden Democrats) is often assigned to this ideological grouping, as well.

Right-wing criticism against diversity is, however, not the only one. It can also – relatively speaking – emanate from the left, mixing liberal, socialist, Marxist, feminist, and republican criticism. In different ways all of these permutations express the general ideas of the Enlightenment. In his *Against the Multicultural Agenda*, Yehudi O. Webster advocates critical thinking instead of production of ideology; *about* good and bad, and not *in favour of* the good and *against* the bad. Rumy Hasan's *Multiculturalism – Some Inconvenient Truths* constitutes a defence of secularism and a criticism against the resignation and relativism of the left.[59] In *From Fatwa to Jihad*, Kenan Malik criticises all kinds of group idealisation and mystification, regardless whether this sentimentalism pertains to the West or to 'non-western' cultures.[60] In *The Politics of Presence*, Anne Phillips claims that 'ethnic representation' is problematic because this representation generally lacks political experience.[61] In *Adskillelsens Politik. Multikulturalisme – ideologi og virkelighed*, Jens-Martin Eriksen and Frederik Stjernfelt argue that this representation rests on a questionable benevolence by the surrounding society ('external protection') along with patriarchal traits of one's own culture ('internal restriction').[62] Moreover, they claim that classic nationalism and diversity are but two expressions of one and the same anti-modern theory. While 'culturalism of the right' puts one's own culture above other cultures, 'culturalism of the left' embraces exotic cultures to the detriment of one's own culture.[63] In *Culture and Equality: An Egalitarian Critique of Multiculturalism*, Brian Barry argues the rhetoric of diversity discourages equality and democracy since it abandons the idea of social change.[64] In *While Europe Slept*, Bruce Bawer argues that multiculturalists have a blind spot regarding the situation of homosexuals.[65] In *Rechtsaussen... und die verfehlten Strategien der Deutschen Linken* (right-wing extremists and the German left's Mistaken Strategy), Wolfgang Kowalsky – socialist, policy advisor at the European Trade Union Confederation in Brussels (ETUC), and author of numerous books on European right-wing extremism – claims that the methods and theories of the left are similar to the right-wing extremism they are attacking.[66] Despite a black-and-white neo-con rhetoric regarding the war in Bosnia, Nick Cohen's *What's Left – How the Left Lost Its Way is* chiefly a left-wing liberal critique against a multicultural left in theoretical crisis. Torben Bech Dyrberg notes a similar crisis. What we are witnessing, he claims, is a shift from 'an old left to a new type of left: from class to identity'.[67]

This left-wing critique has been largely overlooked. Lately, however, a liberal discussion has emerged. Recently, Dilsa Demirbag-Sten and Per Bauhn published a critique against diversity entitled *Till Frihetens försvar: En kritik av den normativa multikulturalismen* (In Defence of Freedom: A Critique of Normative Multiculturalism).[68] In 2004, Leili Falsafi published an explicitly individualistic critique against diversity called *På tal om mångfald* (Speaking about Diversity).[69] In *Välviljans rasism* (The Racism of Good Intentions), Adam Cwejman addresses a dark connection between racism and diversity.[70] In numerous books, such as *Tomhetens triumf* (The Triumph of Emptiness) and *Organisationer, ledning och processer* (Organisations, Leadership and Processes), Mats Alvesson criticised the idea of diversity.[71] A 2011 spring conference headed by the Axel och Margaret

Ax:son Johnsons Foundation was entitled 'Bortom Multikulti' (Beyond Multiculti).[72] A critical discussion against diversity from the left does, in fact, exist – at least from a relative perspective.

In addition, the websites by the names of 'Avpixlat – Den oretuscherade bilden' (Depixelated: The Unretouched Picture) and 'Flashback', both contain critical analysis of diversity and 'political correctness'. The discussion spans the entire field – from left-wing discussions against diversity's perceived atavistic structures, to criticism marked by various forms of radical rightist discourse. Fusing conservatism with modernist analysis, Svenska Tryckfrihetssällskapet (Swedish Association for the Freedom of the Press) is no less evasive.

A comparison between right-wing and left-wing criticisms of diversity brings out important differences. According to the rightist camp, multiculturalism is at heart left-wing, and hence irreconcilable with conservative values. Multiculturalism, Christian right-wing sites argue, is the communism of our time, and no one, Roger Scruton claims, 'versed in the fundamental truths of pessimism' would accept the 'tricks of race-mixing and multiculturalism'.[73] According to the rightist critique, diversity is progressive and egalitarian – in contrast to our 'natural' inequality such as the division between the elite and the general population, or between workers of 'the hand' and workers of 'the brain'. This criticism targets diversity's (in the eyes of the conservative) utopian quest for peaceful co-existence, and not a more disillusioned idea about separate ethnic communities.

Left-wing critique is different. According to the liberal view, diversity is authoritarian, collectivist, and reactionary. Socialist and Marxist critics attack diversity's culturalism, economic naiveté, and lack of concern for the gist of leftist thought – the concept of class. Feminist criticism targets oppression of women within certain minority groups, in particular within Islam. A politically legitimate citizenship within the frames of the nation state is jeopardised, Republican critics argue, by the leader-cult within ethnic minorities. The mirror image of this left-wing critique is, moreover, supported by the fact that diversity, instead of social optimism, is associated with relativism, ethnic defeatism, and latent violence. According to this left-wing critique, diversity is not only linked to conservatism but a case of it.

The distinction between left and right is linked to a basic tenant – the difference between equality and inequality. Equality means that no individual may be singled out based on background; whether given special favours and being wrapped up in a mist of romanticism, or be excluded for any reason but purely professional ones. The Italian political scientist Norberto Bobbio is prominent among those for whom the entire conflict between left and right may be caught in the distinction between equality and inequality.[74]

In Bobbio's analysis, equality is linked to modernity and the endeavour to fight back the structures of privilege of the old class system. At this point I wish to cite the British historian Bernhard Crick who in 1963 was one of the co-founder of the Society against Racial Discrimination at the London School of Economics and Political Science. As the story goes, the British public, Crick declared at the society's official opening ceremony, ought to treat immigrants from ethnic minority groups 'as equals, but not as more than equals'. A member of the audience then wondered who would possibly consider treating immigrants as 'more than equal'.[75] Crick's remark was seen as an arrow without a target. I disagree. Crick's addition is saturated with meaning – it touches the very core of the failure of multiculturalism.

But let us return to the the subject of this book. This is the background: In the late 1990s, Swedish social democracy, and above all Mona Sahlin, former candidate to the Prime Minister post, had started to adopt the idea of mainstream diversity. Subsequently, in October 1999, Thomas Östros – Minister of Education at the time – was authorised to appoint a commissioner with the task of suggesting diversity measures at the university. The purpose was to 'increase diversity regarding (…) ethnic background among students and teachers in order for the university to better reflect diversity in society'.[76] A week later, Boel Flodgren, then Vice Chancellor at Lund University, was appointed Commissioner.[77] In May 2000, a

260-page report entitled: *Mångfald i högskolan – reflektioner och förslag om social och etnisk mångfald vid högskolan (SOU 2000:47)* (Diversity at the university – reflections and suggestions regarding social and ethnic diversity at the university), was presented.[78] *Diversity at the university* (from now on) resulted in a number of 'suggestions and propositions' where the government, among other things, commissioned 'universities and colleges to prepare action plans for ethnic diversity'.[79] The ambition was to turn diversity from a perspective to a norm. In the appropriation letter of the 2002 fiscal year, universities and colleges were, no later than 31 December 2002, required to prepare plans aimed at actively fostering and widening recruitment to the university.[80] Shortly thereafter, all Swedish universities and colleges presented diversity plans. Diversity and multiculturalism had been integrated into Swedish state authorities as well as within the university.

Until now, *Diversity at the University* has not been subject to a more thorough analysis. Regarding multiculturalism in higher education, it is where everything started. But the report's ambitions goes beyond the university. It describes a social trend on the march. Nowhere else is diversity within social democracy more clearly expressed. The fact that the diversity plans were prepared as an explicit response to *Diversity at the University* makes them, on their part, apt companions to the report. A more extensive investigation into these diversity plans has not previously been conducted.

The story of a Social Democratic mantra

In order to understand *Diversity at the University*, two forms of diversity must be distinguished: one with no connection to multiculturalism as a social theory, and another one more or less identical with multiculturalism. While the former version is purely descriptive – i.e. displays the percentage of various groups within a particular society – the latter one is normative by nature. It is not about how things are but the way things *ought to be.* Normative diversity is a quest for a political objective: a multicultural society characterised by diversity.

As a case of the former definition, *Diversity at the University* gives the example of Roth, according to whom a multicultural society is a society containing not only one but many cultures – at times referred to as a multi-ethnic society.[81] According to this 'weak' and descriptive definition, a variety of cultures sharing the same territorial space are defined by 'diversity.'[82]

More often, however, a normative and ambitious approach is being used; diversity, as it were, as a political program. *Diversity at the University* offers a description of Sweden's social transformation over the past few decades: 'For some time now, Sweden has been changing from a society characterised by cultural homogeneity to a more diverse society.'[83] The benefits of this transformation, the report claims, is evident, because never before has our country been bestowed such as fortune of wealth and variety.' As a consequence, Sweden today 'is part of the world to an extent it has never been before'.[84] Presently, 'almost 20 per cent of our population has a background in other countries and cultures'.[85] 'Proper resources', the report continues, 'are required' to ensure that 'the issue of diversity will be dealt with by the university in a more assertive manner'. Therefore, it is suggested, 'the question of diversity at the university must now, in a focused and systematic manner, be top priority'. During an initial five-year project, the university will construct 'a system enabling diversity (...) to increase'.[86] Rich material has been studied, 'interviews, meetings, study visits and seminars' have been conducted in order to 'describe (...) the ethnic diversity at the university', and, showing that this is a case of normative diversity – 'various measures taken in order for it to increase'.[87] Under the heading – 'Contested concepts', this distinction clearly comes to the fore: 'The divergence between descriptive and normative diversity is central: each and every society is somehow marked by diversity, but the essence of this particular dialogue is the extent to which we understand diversity, acknowledge it, and manage to use it properly'.[88] *Diversity at the University*, hence, is more ambitious than merely suggesting a descriptive illustration of a society characterised by diversity. It is a pursuit, and, as will be dealt with below, about political objectives. We must 'understand' diversity, i.e. acknowledge its benefits, and, moreover, 'use it properly'. In its normative and far-reaching interpretation of the concept of diversity, *Diversity at the University* finds support in *Aktiva åtgärder för att främja etnisk mångfald i arbetslivet* (Active measures in order to foster ethnic diversity at work), published by the Ombudsman against ethnic discrimination: 'The ambition to foster ethnic diversity implies much more than merely allowing a certain mix of background among the employees. Recruiting people with an ethnic background hitherto absent is merely an initial measure'. "Above and beyond that', it is claimed, 'ethnic diversity is a question of quality'. Hence, while the endeavour to adjust a work place to where all groups feel represented should be approved, it is still not enough. Ethnic composition is surpassed by a particular quality aspect, according to which diversity 'enables multifaceted ways to take on job assignments'.[89] The definition of diversity in the report is, therefore, chiefly normative. The prevalence of ethnic minorities in Swedish society is not only a statistical fact but, in addition, enriching and in need of increasing. A society with a greater proportion of immigrants is, *in itself*, a better society than one where immigrants are fewer in number. The coming discussion will deal with diversity only in this more ambitious and normative version. This particular form of enrichment by means of diversity, it should be underscored, has nothing to do with influx of ideas, or with any other form of intellectual fertilisation. Intellectualism, i.e. inner variation, richness, pluralism and 'diversity' appears dated; as illustrated by an 'exclusive' Swedish group of students characterised by 'less diversity'.[90] What this is about is the mere physical presence of ethnic minorities and immigrants in Swedish society, and its ostensive beneficial consequences. When the advertisement industry or the university website try to engage a black person, it is not about his or her personality, it is about skin colour.

Let us now return to Bernhard Crick. He insists, as will be remembered, that the idea of equality either works both ways or not at all; neither the domestic population nor new ethnic groups should be given special treatment, whether belittled or idealised, discriminated against or elevated, treated better or worse. What, then, does it mean to say that the issue of diversity must be dealt with in a 'more forceful manner?' – and that it must be a 'top priority'? This means that ethnic minority groups in Sweden are being subject to idealisation and favouritism, and that, moreover, the (supposedly) homogeneous group of indigenous Swedes are being belittled and trivialised. It also means that immigrant groups are put on pedestals because it is assumed that they are considered theoretically inferior to domestic Swedes, while native Swedes are being marginalised because – somehow – it is taken for granted that we – theoretically – are superior. We are expected to be fascinated by their primitive power and animalistic spirit. This exoticism is not new. A long time ago, during their years overseas, Joseph Conrad and George Orwell were both opposed to these imperialistic tendencies, and – by extension – against all kinds of 'colonial craze' among the western upper classes.

The rhetoric of diversity says: we must all be vigilant against our own ethnocentrism. *Diversity at the University* elaborates the same idea from the other end. Now, what must be admitted are no longer our vices but the virtues of diversity. Unless you do that you have failed to understand. To 'acknowledge diversity and use it properly' falls within the same category. In brief: unless you like it, you have made a mistake. The very concept 'acknowledgement' is of particular interest because it is normally not used to enforce appreciation, but to demand mental self-examination. In either case, this is emotional blackmail evoking memories of the Soviet Union. I would not say that *Diversity at the University* tries to manipulate. I do not question the intentions, but the lack of ideological reflection.

Another fact demonstrating that it is actually about normative diversity – and in fact multiculturalism as an ideology – has to do with the historical development from 'less diversity' to 'greater diversity'. 'If', the report maintains, 'it would be fair to say that a previous selection process leading to a relatively exclusive student group, also meant a certain similarity in terms of motives, talent etc. – i.e. less diversity, then, the current situation results in diversity of a considerably higher degree'.[91] Yesterday's Sweden was, in other words, characterised by less diversity.

The emerging image of a 'relatively exclusive group of students' – similar in motive and talent – appears grey and lustreless – almost as intellectually challenged.[92] In comparison, then, today's Sweden stands out as more creative and stimulating, characterised, as it is, by 'greater diversity'. But, of course, you can see it from the other end of the scope. If intellectual resemblance (in, I take it, considerable theoretical aptitude) reduces diversity, diversity of talent (i.e. larger proportion of students less well adjusted to higher education), amounts to more diversity. The task is not, therefore, to acquire richness, pluralism, and 'diversity' in terms of ideas and perspectives, but to obtain ethnic, cultural, religious etc. diversity – and nothing but. The matter of fact is also, worth adding, implicitly recognised in *Diversity at the University*. But this, it is claimed, is more than compensated by an increased ethnic variation. The level of debate goes down while the range of colours goes up, a cynic might say. This inner and previously overlooked tension between theorethical talent and ambition in terms of percentage of teenagers enrolled in university studies (Sweden aims for 50%) must be kept in mind in the discussion below. This is because the report – along with virtually any other document in the area – keeps reiterating that, instead of lowering the quality of higher education, so-called 'widened recruitment' actually 'creates quality', or 'ensures quality'. As I will return to below, the report was 'commissioned to illustrate how diversity can be used in order to raise the level of quality' – which appears to rest on the premise that theoretically talented Swedes must be challenged by ethnic minorities.[93]

The discourse of diversity borrows various ideas from the tradition of modernity, an example being the state's ability to constrain the actions of individuals and the extent to which the majority may hold norm-breakers under control. We will return to this. *Diversity at the University* also, however, expresses various forms of postmodern tendencies, such as regarding the ways in which Swedish institutions may be affected by ethnic minorities. As cited above, ethnic diversity implies 'a multitude of diverse perspectives and ways to tackle the action'. But what this practically means is not explained. The enthusiasm is reminiscent of the one above, where the university clientele to date was compared to the rainbow of diversity. Still, rules apply to public administrations. While 'diversified perspectives' perhaps sound tempting, it may all easily end in lack of efficiency, nepotism, and chaos – features characterising the pre-democratic state, which, worth noting, the modern Swedish civil servant tradition subsequently managed to overcome.

These ideas all originate from the German sociologist Max Weber and his model of bureaucracy: to us of a postmodern age slow and rigid, to Weber safe and ruled by law. The question whether an agency is augmented by any one individual does not depend on his or her background, roots, or any other form of cultural kitsch, but on whether this person is qualified for the job. Diversity rhetoric about creative immigrants illustrates another form of culturist kitsch – the inherent superiority of distant cultures characterised by 'creativity'. A more realistic definition of creativity, however, is that either the legal system has broken down or, indeed, never existed in the first place. Traffic in Hanoi, capital of Vietnam, is creative because it is slow and marred by egotism beyond belief. The upper class left, George Orwell writes, 'does not seem to notice that they are only entertaining the thought that the working class is dirty out of choice and not out of necessity'.[94] The idea that we are furnished with creativity and multifaceted perspectives by ethnic minorities is not only postmodern self-criticism beyond reason. It also expresses an upper-class patronising attitude towards minority cultures, because we are whitewashing our conscience when we depict their improvised desperation as playfulness.

The above argument implies that native Swedes are incapable of 'tackling the action' in innovative ways, as if the transformation leading to a formalised bureaucracy, or Saltsjöbadsavtalet (the Saltsjöbaden Agreement) creating peace and prosperity on the labour market through almost the entire 20th century, somehow does not count. The ethnic minority is seen as superior to native Swedes. Again, Bernhard Crick may be quoted. The ethnic minority is not only our equals, but more than equals. The scheme of master and servant is still standing, but has been turned upside down. In the midst of the mayhem not much has happened.

Postmodernists, the German sociologist Jürgen Habermas writes, are young conservatives, because, he argues, an indifference to those great and demanding social issues – and by extension to social progress as such – dwell behind an air of radicalism. Similarly, arguably, behind paper-thin anti-authoritarianism, diversity rhetoric will result in pre-modern ideas. Certainly, faceless bureaucrats, or, for that matter, Swedish academics of the 1950s all versed in Latin, are easy prey for a nice joke. One may question routines, be creative, break all bureaucratic norms and rules. Still, this kind of no holds-barred self-righteousness is nothing new. All these 'multifaceted perspectives and ways to tackle the action' were all the rage during the 19th century – a time when laws aiming to protect fragile groups were still weak. Behind the dullness of bureaucracy, rule of law applies. Under the mask of colourful creativity and postmodern playfulness, decisions are often arbitrary, constantly favouring those in power. In case *Diversity at the University* expresses the views of a conservative elite, why not say so?

In the above quotation, 'ethnic diversity is also a matter of quality'. This statement shows that this is a case of normative diversity. But the ambition to connect quality to diversity is also quintessential in *Diversity on the University.* In this matter, diversity is defended. Three cases might illustrate. First: What does this link between diversity and quality generally look like? Second: You cannot assess quality unless you have comparative evidence. Does this exist and what does it say? Third: The report was commissioned to show that diversity increases quality in higher education. What was this about?

Under '1.1 Mission and method of the report', aspect 4, 'How to handle diversity in a quality-augmenting manner', *Diversity at the University* is to 'give examples (...) where quality of education is increased as a result of the proper use of ethnic diversity.'[95] Under 'Measures in order to increase diversity', a 'few examples' are suggested 'in order to utilise diversity and hence boost quality'.[96] Moreover, included under the diversity aspect is, as stated in a status report, the issue of how to make use of diversity in higher education in order to increase quality in the organisation.[97] As 'ethnic diversity increases, it is vital to take proper measures in order to ensure above all the teaching quality in higher education'.[98] This quote is to be found under the headline 'More diversity – more quality', a section also containing the following sentences: 'In a multicultural university diversity can be used to boost quality', and the utilising of diversity should, then, 'constitute a natural aspect in a much needed augmentation of pedagogic competence at the university'.[99]

Under 'Diversity work as part of quality assessment', we find 'Diversity as part of quality', along with the following additional two action-oriented points: 'Resources for pedagogic diversity' and 'The developing of background material in order to show how diversity can be utilised to support quality in teaching, research and administration'.[100] 'During the coming five-year-period, diversity must', it is furthermore claimed in the report, 'be an area of priority in quality assessment at the university'.[101] Ethnic diversity must therefore be regarded as a 'criterion of quality regarding the recruitment of students, composition of staff (and) teaching (...) in future quality assessments (...), as well as in university assessments, and in assessments of courses and programs'.[102] The ambition is to engage the university, because the undertaking 'of quality criteria ought to be conducted in close proximity to universities and colleges'.

An important outcome of the report was to suggest that the government, in order to support the quality aspect above, should 'put aside considerable ear-marked funds – approximately SEK 500 million (USD 80 million) – by means of which universities (...), during this five-year period, could fund their development and pilot tasks'.[103] Immediately thereafter, the report continues, the authorities are recommended to 'consider whether the supply of financial resources should vary in relation to the success of fostering diversity'.[104] At the universities, these recommendations gave rise to expectations of substantial financial support.

Diversity at the University stresses numerous links between diversity and quality. Information about the benefits of diversity is needed within 'staff training', such as 'leadership courses'; in 'education for students, councillors and administrators, the merits of diversity is required', and in a global world without boundaries 'ethnic diversity in education, among students and teachers instantly boost quality'.[105]

These largely emotional links between diversity and quality aside, the connection between them is also supported by arguments. Three of them will be presented below. The first argument relies on a broad definition of diversity as a concept. As stated in the report, there is an aspect 'in the relationship between diversity and quality that needs stressing. At the university, successful research and education is preconditioned by a diversity of perspectives, i.e. enabling a variety of voices and the co-existence of a variety of openly contesting perspectives'. Therefore, the report concludes, 'diversity's positive effects on quality go without saying'.[106] The second argument can be found in the report's introductory 'Summary'. Under 'Diversity in quality work', the 'social dimension' is addressed, according to which, more diversity leads to improved quality because 'cultural diversity is a good thing'. Cultural variety in higher education 'leads to multicultural and multisocial understanding and reduces ethnic prejudices'.[107] As a third and final argument, the report shifts the discussion to the issue of general societal acceptance, something it insists the university must take into consideration: 'Within the framework of the social quality dimension, societal approval of the university is aided by ethnic (...) diversity'.[108] The mixing of cultures reduces intolerance, which increases societal acceptance. Hence, diversity leads to quality.

Still, comparisons over time must be questioned. It is, the report admits, 'most difficult and perhaps not meaningful to make a comparison between higher education in the 1950s with the present situation, where the number of students has multiplied ten-fold'.[109] Elsewhere, the report distinguishes between the level of formal education and the level of the knowledge as such: 'During the 20th century, we have witnessed a remarkable rise in formal education. Whether this also has resulted in a corresponding increase in knowledge is, however, uncertain.' 'Probably', it is concluded, 'this cannot be measured scientifically because knowledge at different times on such as long time scale is most likely impossible to compare'.[110]

But there are things to be said about this. As seen above, diversity is to be utilised to 'increase' and 'augment' quality. *Diversity at the University* is rich with similar phrases. 'Diversity' appears about 500 times in 125 pages – i.e. about four times per page – and the link to quality is constantly reiterated. As a comparison, a communist during the Stalin era, the author Arthur Koestler recalls, mentions 'Lenin' in his 480-page book 'almost one hundred times'.[111] The social democratic report surpasses the loyalty of a totalitarian state 20 times over.

What, then, a few lines up, does it mean when diversity is to be 'utilised'? It means to not let things go to waste. Quality, in other words, is inherent in diversity the way iron can be extracted from ore. 'A report is to be drawn to show how diversity can be utilised in a quality-enhancing manner'. Leaving aside the awkward nature of the sentence, the message is merely a matter of execution. Something to be dealt with in a certain direction, and something else has to be prepared for it. Unless you can show that diversity fosters quality, you have failed. The psychological violence is right under the surface. Among students and teachers diversity 'instantly' leads 'to higher quality'. As stated in the report, the university was supposed to be part of the process of connecting diversity and quality. Then again, the social democratic government was recommended to distribute financial resources in accordance with 'success in fostering diversity'. As it seems, funding of the university was the result of the extent to which diversity could be associated with quality. This combination of participation and lack of self-determination reminds me of a comment during an interview with Anders Persson, one of the authors of the report. Questioned about the autonomy of the university, Persson answered with a twist: 'Your intellectual independence is undisputed, as long as you can make a living'.[112]

As an argument in support of the association between diversity and quality, *Diversity at the University* introduces the idea of 'diversity of perspectives', meaning that 'different voices can take part, and 'many perspectives co-exist, allowed to freely interact'. Therefore, the conclusion goes, 'the fact that diversity boosts quality is plain to see'[113] The concept of 'voices' should not, at this point, be misunderstood. In the ideology of diversity, voices do not refer to individual voices, but to the rights of the ethnic groups as a homogeneous entity. This is one of the core features of diversity as a social program, in accordance with any other strongly collectivist social model. If the concept is widened so as to encompass individual voices as well, the entire ideology of diversity would be undermined. Although diversity counts among its followers, numerous self-professed liberals (caused, Rumy Hasan argues, by 'the liberal post-Colonial guilt') the relation between diversity and liberalism is – at least on a doctrinal level – antagonistic.[114] Striving for ethnic mobilisation and group rights, early multiculturalists fought against – precisely – the 'liberal illusion' of the 1950s about 'one person, one vote'. Today's critics of multiculturalism claim that individuals within ethnic minority groups are being repressed and neglected; individuals whose perspectives and voices are forgotten. When *Diversity at the University*, then claims that it is 'very easy' to support the idea of diversity because it enables discussion and individual freedom, it is either cynical or naive. Why tick all the boxes on the chart, instead of acknowledging diversity's benefits and shortcomings at face value and insist on the virtues of collectivism and the menace of individualism the way conservatives and Marxists – openly and honestly – have always done?

The 'voice' of the ethnic group, then, does not belong to the individual. Who or what is behind it? It is the ethnic representative, or community leader. This arrangement is highly conservative and in essence patriarchal because female ethnic representatives rarely occur. Moreover, the idea is closely associated with (right-wing) populist/organic kitsch: the leader as head tormented by troubles, and the people as fingertips – silent, reacting limbs. More still, this representative borrows features from fascism and the idea of the worker of the 'mind' as opposed to the worker of the 'hand'; from history mysticism, pessimism, and related forms of political romanticism. It is not clear why this kind of political idealism would ensure quality in higher education.

Previously, it was noted that 'increased diversity contributes to higher quality because cultural diversity is a good thing'.[115] It is good because 'it contributes to multicultural (...) understanding and reduces ethnic prejudices'.[116] The idea is that racism, xenophobia, and prejudices are reduced when cultures are mixed and intertwined. Proximity creates mutual bonds, leading to communication and shared understanding. On a general level, the idea has something to it; if only we listen to other people we might understand them better. But some actually argue the opposite: that 'cultural blending' sharpens antagonism, increases the support for extremist parties, and that the only way out is to allow for a certain separation between various ethnic groups. This conclusion is common among those who have studied the conflict between Israel and Palestine. Scholars of European right-wing populism and extremism are equally distributed in both camps.

Studies of the French Front National or the Freedom Party in Austria, tend to show that our voting pattern only slightly depends on whether we live near immigrants or not. There is a near zero correlation between proximity to immigrant groups and voting preference. However, the mechanisms behind these attitudes appear to differ. Support for Sverigedemokraterna (Sweden Democrats), as a concrete example, is not lower in Landskrona (interspersed with immigrant groups), as opposed to Bunkeflostrand (with a more homogeneous Swedish population) – perhaps even slightly higher. As opposed to possibly more cultural and elitist reasons behind a support for Sverigedemokraterna prevailing in Bunkeflostrand, the vote from the low-income in Landskrona (slight stereotype) is probably determined by economic factors. *Diversity at the University* has 260 pages, including attachments. Still, the question of proximity and right-wing support is conspicuously absent. The report argues that diversity contributes to equality because 'cultural blending is a good thing'. None other than a right-wing fanatic would claim that cultural blending is a bad thing. Why, then, is it uncontroversial to be stereotypical top-down? I thought the report was aimed for an audience in higher education.

It is said that blending of cultures reduces 'ethnic prejudices' – i.e. misunderstandings and precipitated conclusions.[117] It is about psychology. All will be fine, if only we live close to each other. We are witnessing a mirror image of the 'ethno-pluralism' of *Nouvelle Droite* – the reckless pessimism of the French new right, proclaiming that we cannot live together because foreign cultures will be 'subject to the brutal rites of assimilation', while our own culture, by this alien influx, will be thinned out into oblivion.[118] This mirror image insists: We can always live together because this will lead to cross-breeding of ideas and fruitful co-existence and a diversity of voices. With a pat on your shoulders and a few words about the virtues of cultural blending, you get your former camp guard as neighbour. Militant pessimism is replaced by militant enthusiasm. Reality is elsewhere. While all our suspicious are true, claims the right-wing extremist, they are all prejudices, the multiculturalist shoots back. We are either whipped into antagonism or flogged into concord. It is difficult to see the difference.

By sharing the same territory with strangers, the report insists, racism is prevented and quality enhanced. But one might just as well insist on the opposite: Diversity, by itself, *does not* lead to quality. The precondition for a smooth and vibrant society is *not* constituted by ethnic heterogeneity but by ethnic homogeneity – the fact that we do *not* differ from each other.

Robert Putnam's *E Pluribus Unum: Diversity and Community in the Twenty-first Century* is an important recent defence of this idea.[119] This study, based on empirical data from the 2000 *The Social Capital Community Benchmark Survey*, contains about 30,000 observations ranging over 41 American societies.[120]

As an icon for right-wingers, Putnam does not quite make sense. While some might seek to exploit him, he *does not* say that immigration is a bad thing. 'Generally', he argues, 'immigration and heterogeneous societies appear to foster creativity',[121] and he supports this idea by citing sources where ethnic diversity tends to fuel workgroup creativity.[122] In particular, this pertains to diversity and variation of an *intellectual nature.*[123] In the long run, Putnam believes that the net effects of immigration and diversity are positive, not in the least in the US, his own country. But, then, what about 'social trust' and 'social capital' – i.e. solidarity and social cohesion? How are they affected by ethnic diversity? That is the question.

Putnam brings up two models. According to the 'contact hypothesis', interethnic tolerance and understanding are amplified by diversity. Contact and interaction lead to trust. In support of this, Putnam quotes a study on American soldiers during World War II, where mutual suspicion was less pronounced in mixed platoons as opposed to in all-white ones.[124]

'For progressives', Putnam acknowledges, 'the contact theory is alluring'. But, he continues, 'I think it is fair to say that most (though not all) empirical studies have tended instead to support the so-called 'conflict theory', which suggest that, for various reasons – but above all, contention over limited resources – diversity fosters out-group distrust and in-group solidarity'. The more we are brought into contact with people with another background, the more we tend to stick to 'our own' group.[125] Across work-groups in the West, internal heterogeneity is more often than not associated with lower group cohesion, lower satisfaction, and higher turnover.[126] Across countries in the West, ethnic heterogeneity appears to be linked to lower social trust and less sense of solidarity.[127] On a more local level, greater ethnic diversity is associated with lower social trust and in some cases lower investment in public goods.[128] In America, across census tracts – statistical subdivisions of a county, more pronounced ethnic heterogeneity is associated with lower rates of car-pooling – a 'social practise that embodies trust and reciprocity'.[129] Interracial trust is rather high in homogeneous South Dakota and lower in San Francisco and Los Angeles. 'The more ethnically diverse the people we live among, the less, Putnam maintains, 'we trust them'. Normatively, he admits, this is distressing, but 'it seems to be consistent with conflict theory'.[130] Mats Alvesson reaches similar conclusions: 'Diversity, and this is of course the gist of the problem, brings all kinds of disagreements, conflicts and dissenting views, and this is not easy to handle'. A concerned supervisor says: 'You know, we can all feel good because we are part of a happy multicultural family, and the company will profit in all sorts of ways from it. The truth is another story. If people really are different there will be conflicts, they want to have it their way, and will be upset of somebody else tells them how things should be done…'[131]

But Putnam's conclusions do not simply adhere to 'conflict theory'. The distrust caused by ethnic diversity does not only affect those who do not look like us, but also those who do. Ethnic diversity seems 'to trigger *not* in-group/out-group division, but anomie or social isolation'. In ethnically diverse surroundings, people appear to 'hunker down', that is pull in, much like turtles.[132] In sociology, the anomie and loneliness associated with *Gesellschaft,* big cities, and constantly being surrounded by strangers is merely a scientific observation. Ferdinand Tönnies and Émile Durkheim have written extensively about this.[133]

Also other aspects of social trust and civic engagement are, Putnam claims, negatively correlated with diversity, such as lower trust in local government, local leaders, and the local news media; lower trust in one's own political influence, lower political participation (i.e. voting); less expectation that others will work together to solve collective concerns (such as energy or water shortages); fewer close friends; less happiness and lower perceived life quality; more time spent in front of the TV-set, and more agreement that 'television is my most important form of entertainment'.[134] With a shorter social distance, says Putnam, trust and cooperation come easier. Then, 'there is a feeling of common identity, closeness, and shared experience. But when social distance is great, people perceive and treat the other as belonging to a different category. Even after a long acquaintance, there are still feelings of apprehension and reserve'.[135] 'Social distance', Putnam adds, 'depends in turn on social identity: our sense of who we are.'[136]

Tolerance towards difference, he sums up, 'is but a first step'. To strengthen a sense of mutual understanding and shared identities, 'we need more opportunities for meaningful interaction across ethnic lines where Americans (new and old) work, learn, play, and live'.[137] The challenge is not to 'make "them" like "us", but rather "by creating a new, more accommodating sense of "we"; a reconstruction of diversity that does not bleach out ethnic specificities, but creates overarching identities that ensure that those specificities do not trigger the allergic, "hunker down" reactions.'[138] In a similar fashion, the Polish sociologist Zygmunt Bauman claims, we must seek to foster a common sense of community, and try to avert the rise of particularist and potentially disintegrating groupings.[139]

'Scientific examinations of issues related to diversity are at times', Putnam argues, 'inflamed as the result of research become part of the contemporary political debate'. It would, he says, 'be unfortunate if a politically correct progressivism were to deny the reality of the challenge to social solidarity posed by diversity'. Notably, he adds, it 'would be equally unfortunate if a historical and ethnocentric conservatism were to deny that addressing that challenge is both feasible and desirable'. To mention multicultural progressivism in tandem with ethnocentric conservatism might seem puzzling. But in fact, this statement captures the essence of the present discussion. This book is a critique against myopic, self-righteous conservatism *under the guise of* progressive ideas.[140]

In support of his point of view, Putnam quotes the then Democratic Senator Barack Obama. While acknowledging the inherent value of cultural belonging, this must not, Obama maintains, 'determine people's life chances and there is no sense of superiority or inferiority [...]'. If 'we can expand that attitude to embrace (all our various backgrounds), then [...] all our kids can feel comfortable with the worlds they come from, knowing they are part of something larger'.[141]

As already mentioned, Putnam is a bad icon for right-wingers. Still, he has on occasion been used as one, at least regarding this paper. At the same time, he has been silenced or criticised for the wrong reasons by the left-liberal establishment. Then again, he is sometimes surprisingly cautious. At least in two cases he could have sharpened the argument further. Creativity in work-groups, he maintains, is fostered by diversity – in particular diversity of an *intellectual nature.*[142] Intellectual diversity, then, becomes a subsection of ethnic diversity. At first sight, it looks like a reasonable attempt to rescue an intellectually discredited ideology of diversity. Still, ethnic diversity and intellectual pluralism need to be carefully separated from one another. Multicultural diversity is by nature visual. It is all about a 'mosaic', or 'rainbow' of skin colour, hair colour, body shape, and 'phrenological qualities'. On top of this, multicultural diversity is collectivistic because the individual is not autonomous but invariably legitimised by something beyond itself – background, history, recognition, representation, identification, roots, sense of community, protection, security, belonging etc. Diversity, then, *is not* about inner personal qualities: preferences, values, and judgments and ideas, convictions, mental predispositions, personality, psychological character traits – i.e. all those qualities that, added together, make up intellectual diversity. Multicultural diversity is visual and collectivistic, not individualistic and abstract. To borrow Martin Luther King's classic phrase, intellectual diversity is 'colour blind'. While it would be unfair – and a case of classic racism – to hold the view that intellectual enrichment is best made by 'us', anyone to whom intellectual diversity is a subcategory to ethnic diversity merely puts this intolerant scheme on its head. Quoting Crick again: 'We should treat the immigrant as our equal but not as more than that.'

By separating diversity and *intellectual* diversity, the former is stripped naked. Those specifically human traits, traits that we do *not* share with other species, e.g. the capacity for abstract thinking, individualism, creativity, discipline, self-consciousness, are precisely the ones excluded in the multicultural equation. Instead focus is exclusively on our physiological, bodily, group-based features – in other words all those qualities that make it impossible to say: this signifies a human being. Given this multicultural fixation on our bodily packaging, we can not explain human history ever since the rise of language and abstract thinking about 100,000 years ago. Moreover, it is pointless to speak about diversity of an intellectual nature because intellectualism presupposes a richness and variety of ideas, self-criticism, a tentative approach to one's conclusions, etc.

In addition, diversity's optimistic contact-hypothesis should have been subject to a somewhat more thorough discussion. As will be remembered, Putnam brings up an old study of the US Army, where interaction between racially distinct soldiers was more relaxed compared to segregated platoons. In Putnam's eyes – and I could not agree more – this example from the racial segregation of the 1940s is 'remarkable' and a striking argument in favour of multicultural social engineering. America in the 1940s was an apartheid system – a most sinister kind of cultural separation – in which, evidently, the army could ease tensions between groups. Constantly stressing cultural distinctions is, then again, not a risk-free endeavour. In contemporary ethnicity discourse, two students from different countries socialising invariably comes under the name of a 'meeting of cultures', and it touches base in literature as yet another case in favour of the contact hypothesis. The class-based analysis of the classic left has gone missing. Rather than distinguished by cultural 'roots', students are better, as noted by Pierre Bourdieu and others, characterised by shared class interests – academic area studied, social status, aesthetic taste, table manners, and so on. Classic Marxists would probably be puzzled at the sight of this multicultural enthusiasm, because, they would claim, the academic classes always had common interests. What is the point of driving a cultural wedge between young people who might have other things on their mind than their respective cultural heritage? Why not just leave them alone? Unless there is something to bridge, the multicultural conflict hypothesis does not really prove much. As uneventful as it looks, perhaps the truth is that the contact hypothesis is valid when cultural distance is short and bridged by common language and social status while the conflict hypothesis applies when the cultural distance is longer. To talk about hypotheses is perhaps stretching it.

When diversity protagonists pride themselves on bridging ethnic divides there is often a combination of pessimism, economic calculation, and misconceived self-image. Only by manufacturing sentimental visions about ethnic conflicts is it possible to bring these conflicts to a peaceful conclusion by means of successful multiculturalism. The more dramatic tensions on sale, the more righteous and necessary diversity appears. We are witnessing a multicultural self-playing piano.

A few years ago, in an interview with Peter Sichrowsky, the then General Secretary of Jörg Haider's Freedom Party and a Jew, Sichrowsky declared, 'The Holocaust is not as important among today's secular Jews as many wish to believe.'[143] Apart from those who are honestly engaged in Jewish affairs, others merely exploit Jewish suffering for selfish motives.[144] On occasion, multiculturalism is no less of an emphatic industry where fictitious walls are being erected as a means to boost your career.

The multicultural contact hypothesis claims that cultural depths and authenticity may be overcome by means of 'peaceful co-existence'. But why should group conflicts always be reduced by proximity? Would it not rather underscore an existential distance? In Sweden, we are taught never to expect other cars to adjust to your needs. Never change lanes and rely on other cars to accommodate. In Hanoi traffic, this rule is key. Why should knowledge about this particular difference deepen an understanding between Sweden and Vietnam? Perhaps, at times, we would be better off if we would think that our rules apply everywhere? Perhaps tolerance and emotional intimacy, on occasion, are preconditioned by a certain amount of ethnocentrism and ignorance?

The contact hypothesis always accompanies those Western multiculturalists who are inspired by exotic, cultural expressions from overseas. A genuine interest in Balinese culture is like any other interest. But why should close encounters with exotic cultures inevitably result in fanning interest? Our 'colonial craze' – whether it is dance, handicrafts, or food – tends to fade away the moment something more heartfelt is discovered. This particular form of multicultural interest is ecstatic, superficial, and ephemeral – an example of the cultural shopping mall of postmodernity. It precisely characterises those who advocate for 'cultural understanding'. Yet again, I wish to draw attention to Bernhard Crick's statement about the inherent worth of equality *as a principle*. Either it works both ways or it does not apply at all. Why must individuals from overseas be enchanted by our customs? Why can they not be aghast at the sight of us eating rotten fish or get bored or amused when we jump around a fir tree like frogs in the dead of winter?

Still, multiculturalists fail to be impressed by these concerns. They feel their views are confirmed regardless of the outcome of their racial-bridging efforts. Either cross-ethnic interaction occurs and lends support to the multiculturalist contact hypothesis, or it fails to do so, confirming their gloomy perception of the Swedish native population. Either understanding comes with proximity or Sweden is characterised by structural racism.

The connection between diversity and quality – as presented in *Diversity at the University* – can be further questioned by the fact that the report is unwilling to compare quality over time: These efforts, it is claimed, are 'probably not meaningful', and knowledge over time is 'most likely (…) incompatible'.[145] Undeniably, this is not easy, in particular due to the recent rapid expansion of the Swedish university system. But why not give it a try? The statistical material is just lying there. This lack of interest is all the more puzzling due to the fact that *Diversity at the University* is the product of an organisational culture characterised by – in the words of Lennart Lundqvist – 'quality assessment mania'.[146] 'It remains to be seen whether today's universities are in terms of quality, superior to those of yesterday.[147] But how, then, can you be so sure that diversity brings quality in higher education?

Formally, universities were supposed to show that diversity was quality-enhancing. What did this mean? *Diversity at the University* was a commissioned by the then Social Democratic government. Under '1.3 Perspectives and premises', the report 'was supposed to show how diversity could be used in order to increase quality'[148] In *Committee directive – Social and ethnic diversity at the university* – the 1999 document preceding *Diversity at the University* – the mission is clearly stated: A special investigator is called upon to illustrate 'how diversity can be used as a quality-boosting factor'.[149]

There was no choice. This had nothing to do with research questions – *if* diversity fostered quality, and, if so, *why*? Instead, it was a matter of execution. The link was taken for granted – the question was *how*. We have already touched upon the fact that the authors were somewhat caught in a mental straight-jacket. Unless they managed to show diversity's positive effects on quality, they had failed. As an extra bonus, the Social Democratic government had announced it ought to be 'assessed whether supply of resources' should 'vary according to the extent of diversity success'.[150] There was not much room to manoeuvre; it was a political task to be completed. As admitted by Anders Persson, one of the authors of the report: 'When you are commissioned by a university vice chancellor, you are well advised to accept it'.[151] Boel Flodgren, the special investigation commissioner, was sitting in the same boat. What if, I asked, she had declined the offer? 'It is hard', Persson replied, 'to disobey the voice of the government'.[152] It was, in its own way, a kind of pecking order: the Social Democratic government commissioned Flodgren and her staff who presented *Diversity at the University*, in which universities were commissioned to 'prepare material to show how diversity – in education, research and administration – could be used in a quality-enhancing way'; and the universities, in turn, launched diversity plans, the content of which were expected to be executed by us researchers and lecturers, no questions asked.[153]

At the same time, Swedish academics are not bound hand and foot. Why, when everything was smacked with ideology, did Boel Flodgren not chose to decline the offer and face the consequences? When part of the mission was to ignore the analytical disparity between class and ethnicity? When it was all a purely political decision made by the Social Democratic government under Göran Persson and Mona Sahlin? Whatever happened to academic integrity? The link between ethnicity and quality, Persson says, was just 'a political thing. The government was behind it'. Asked: 'What was your role in it?' He replied: 'It was a mantra.' 'I can't find any evidence in support of a connection between ethnicity and quality, no statistics or anything else. How do you defend it?' 'We don't', Persson replies.[154]

Persson's experience is particularly interesting. In spring 2001, he published a critical article about the report. 'Perhaps I am unfair', he writes, 'but from my cynical (...) point of view, it appears nowadays more important to *launch* an investigation than to cater for its results'. Time pressure, he says, was a factor: 'In what way is it possible to investigate an issue of such decisive and wide-ranging nature as ethnic diversity (...) in higher education in no more than seven months? What is lost when *Swedish Governments Official Reports* are turned into *Swedish Governments Opinionated Reports*?' Above all, he writes, 'critical reflection is sacrificed'. Another reason why the report was so uncritical, he adds, was because it was assumed that the authors agreed that 'the immigrant's situation in Sweden in any ways was deeply problematic'. From the perspective of the Social Democratic government, this was greatly beneficial, because the report was commissioned to execute an idea that was ideological and could not be empirically proven. One can only speculate about the outcome of an open and unconditional discussion. Imagine if there had not been a report at all. Perhaps multiculturalism would have failed to acquire hegemonic status in higher education. According to mainstream Swedish 'immigration discourse', immigrants are being marginalised by Swedish xenophobia and 'structural racism', while multiculturalists seek to oppose ethnic stereotyping. 'However', Persson claims, 'it can easily be argued that the reason why these ethnic stereotypes exist in the first place is because they are of our making'. 'But this', he says, 'is not because of some ethnicity, but because it is "diversity practise" – a particular routine in handling "immigrant issues" going back decades, and as the result of which immigrants are separated, distinguished, and given special treatment.' In this sense, Persson challenges the rhetoric of diversity. Anti-immigrant stereotyping, he insists, is not alleviated as a result of this rhetoric, but intensified. The fact that the right-wing stereotype revolves around hatred while the stereotype of the multiculturalist is sentimental-romantic does not change much. No one – neither the domestic population nor immigrants – should be put aside, celebrated or denigrated. No one group, Bernhard Cricks insists, should be given privileges.

In the eyes of diversity advocates, the world is 'multifaceted' and yet they cannot wait to divide human beings into collectivist caricatures. Perhaps, after all, diversity does not breed quality but segregation and alienation. Persson's lucid comment about a counter-productive 'diversity discourse' is a good example of something which in his eyes the report is lacking – namely critical reflection.[155] Another concept missing in the report is the conflict hypothesis Putnam refers to above. A critical discussion about a right-wing clichéd conflict hypothesis is thereby neglected. With great zest, racism is under attack, but the mechanisms behind it is of no interest.

If instead, university lecturers had been asked whether diversity leads to quality most of us would probably have answered no. With more quotas and more students with language difficulties, the lower the quality of education. Suppose the Social Democratic government squarely had admitted that quality is *jeopardised* by diversity, but had added that current levels of education must be protected at all cost – what would the response have been like? Probably a sense of great relief and genuine enthusiasm. Instead we are faced with a report arguing that quality is brought and retained by diversity, while in fact, diversity constitutes an imminent threat to quality, and higher education is put in permanent crisis and consternation.

Here, we should add a comment by Perry Anderson who argues that diversity can never, acquire the same status as freedom and equality. Even if the concept intuitively is tempting – such as in 'variation is the spice of life' – it is logically void. The Third Reich brought diversity to European politics, but still failed to bring any good. Nature analogies – such as 'nature is characterised by diversity' – also fail to convince. As has been pointed out by both Voltaire and Friedrich Nietzsche, nature is a morally indifferent master.

While the multiculturalist might call it peaceful co-existence, it is often a blind struggle for survival – 'survival of the fittest'. If nature tells us anything at all about diversity, it is that existence is brutal and characterised by constant antagonism. At the freezing temperature, a naked human body shuts down within twenty minutes. Society – including all its institutions and systems – is largely a revolt *against* blind nature. To invoke diversity in nature is political primitivism.[156]

This shapter showed that the first part of the expression 'Diversity brings quality' is problematic. But what about 'quality'? One possible interpretation would be that percentage x manages test y specified as z. But we do not know. The only example I have come across is a case of postmodern relativism: 'Quality is not fixed but varies': science means different things in different countries, and quality 'also varies over time'.[157] It sounds tolerant but it comes with a cost: diversity – something we fail to define – leads to quality – something we are only vaguely familiar with. Still, higher education in Sweden does have a criterion of quality. It goes under the name of 'genomströmningshastighet' (the speed of flowing through) i.e. pushing students through the system at maximum speed. It tells you about the number of graduating students, but nothing about the quality of education. Quality goes down and hence it goes up.

On ethnic reflection and how to gain public recognition

Above, I discussed the idea of 'general public recognition'. 'Within the societal quality dimension, *Diversity at the University* declares, 'increased ethnic (...) diversity enables an increased societal legitimacy of the university'.[158] By associating diversity and quality, the university gains public acceptance. A similar phrase is found in the document preceding *Diversity at the University*, the 1999 *Kommittédirektiv – Social och etnisk mångfald i högskolan* (Committee directive – Social and ethnic diversity in the university). It states that 'in order for the university to better reflect societal diversity', diversity among students must increase.[159] Before discussing this, a few additional examples will be presented.

A citation in verbatim from the *Kommittédirektiv* opens up the later report. The task was to 'increase diversity in relation to (...) ethnic background among students and teachers to enable the university to better reflect diversity in society'.[160] According to statistical data, 'Administrative personnel is more often recruited among people with a Swedish background'.[161] Hence, we are witnessing 'a kind of administrative marginalisation of people with a foreign background'.[162] A kind of nationalist appointment procedure is, one might argue, replaced by a Eurocentric equivalent: 'Among non-natives, Europe is clearly first, while people from Africa and Asia are under-represented in relation to their percentage of the population'.[163] The idea is borrowed from optics – representation must be mirrored by percentage; some groups are overrepresented, others are under-represented.

However, a mirror metaphor is more common. We are told that the university, 'fails in terms of the societal quality dimension'. This is because 'the ethnic (...) diversity in society is not mirrored at the university.'[164] In light of society's ethnic diversity, three areas are of particular significance:

1. Diversity among students and staff, a reflection of societal diversity.

2. The inherent worth of higher education in a multicultural society because its reflexive character may spark greater cultural acceptance.

3. The enhanced value of independent and critical individuals situated in an identity-political field of tension between individuals, groups, and society.[165]

The university is assessed 'in the light of ethnic diversity in society', and the idea that higher education ought to mirror society's diversity is a recurring theme.[166] The report also has plenty of concrete suggestions to increase the mirror effect between university and society. In order to acquire a 'local reflection of research, teaching and administrative experience of (...) diversity in higher education (...), multiculturalists have launched '"diversity seminars" in close cooperation with six universities'.[167]

On occasion, the critique is more serious. One example is the 'ethnic hierarchy' which currently characterises Sweden and is related to a faulty mirror effect. An 'ethnic division of labour' is being established, 'reflecting an ethnic hierarchy', which, in turn, 'affects how people live and work in our society.'[168] *Diversity at the University* repeatedly reiterates a sliding scale of exclusion, from an appointment procedure plagued by nationalism to one marred by euro centrism – leading on to a routine where individuals from the West are favoured: 'In this hierarchy the Swedes hold the top rung, followed closely by Americans and West Europeans, and on the bottom rung you find individuals from West Asia and Africa'.[169]

Apart from this mirror metaphor, the report refers to 'representation in a society'. It claims that this concept enables all groups to study at the university and as a consequence, is seen as a weapon against the old-school system of class privileges. Initially having established that the university 'structurally is assigned a central role in society,[170] it is emphasised that 'the university also takes the lead as being centre stage in society in terms of ethnic representation'.[171] Even though this summary considers only *ethnic* diversity, there is a variety of others too: ‘In the long run, our ambition must be to implement all forms of diversity: social, ethnic, gender, age, geographic and in numerous other relevant aspects. We must seek to eradicate any obstacle that might stop individuals who wish and are able to study in higher education’, and, the report continues, ‘university staff must also better reflect society's ethnic mix.’[172] The report has great ambitions concerning diversity.

Under ‘Representation in society’, discussions on the ‘identification person’ are also outlined; a privileged individual in a certain group and a spokesperson for other group members. ‘Teaching role models’, the report maintains, are ‘of great value in teaching’, and ‘the prospects of finding one’s proper identification person in an increasingly diverse student group is enhanced by ethnic diversity’.[173] ‘The question of diversity’, it states elsewhere, ‘is a complex one and relates to the university’s diversity in relation to society, as well as other aspects of diversity’.[174] ‘The fact that the university must reflect society at large’, the report continues, ‘also means that the employees have to do it. This is of particular importance among lecturers, because teaching quality, among other things, depends upon to what extent students are able to ”recognize themselves” in the teacher’.[175]

But what, then, is the deeper meaning in this? When does one ‘feel affiliated to’ another human being? In her analysis of Karl Marx, the British political scientist Margaret Canovan makes the observation that human existence, according to Marx, is primarily determined by economic circumstances and primary human needs such as food and sleep. Canovan continues that Marx slightly overlooks the species-specifics for human beings because animals, too, need food and rest. Our intellectual faculties single out human beings. ‘I believe’, Anton Chekhov writes, ‘in carriages with springs, beautiful carpets, and conversations with a certain mental acumen’. Canovan concludes that Marx’s theories are partly based on reactionary, if not outright animalistic premises, despite his progressive reputation.[176]

The idea of ethnic representation in the report can be criticised along similar lines. According to the idea of reflecting society, we recognise those who look like we do. It is all about visual resemblance, such as facial features and skin colour. Animals, too, and this is the problem, identify in this fashion. The flock is united by means of significant traits while showing distance towards the outsider. Unless somebody looks the way I do, I cannot recognise myself because I cannot 'see myself reflected'. While Marx may be labelled a primitivist in the sense that he emphasised qualities unspecific to human beings, the multiculturalists behind *Diversity at the University* are primitivists because they overlook the fact that you can recognise yourself in others also through what they say. With whom do you feel close? Those who look like you, or those who think like you do? Is it about ideas or merely about physical presence? Who is supposed to represent us in Parliament, in the student council, or in local government? Somebody with whom we share political views, or somebody who shares our historical background and skin colour? There are no dissidents in Iran, in case roots speak louder than politics.

The report does actually cite critical material, but on these occasions, it is mostly name-dropping. For instance, Yehudi O. Webster argues in *Against the Multicultural Agenda*, that students should not be taught 'cultural differences, but rather *about* cultural differences and similarities'.[177] What counts is, at the end of the day, not our cultural outfit but our views and opinions. Webster is opposed to interest groups (be it companies, anti-drug campaigns, or lobby organisations) trying to manipulate the students to say the right things.

Instead, he proposes a program in critical thinking, in other words to think *about* good and right, and *about* evil and wrong. Everything must be subject to scientific scrutiny. It is knowledge for its own sake.[178] Webster's clear clarion call for intellectual decency fails to leave any mark in *Diversity at the University*, other than, perhaps, a scent of international glamour.

Jerome Black and Aleem Lakhani have studied the question of ethnic representation and identification in the Canadian parliament in Ottawa. They are both puzzled by the mystification surrounding this ostensibly progressive idea. As Black and Lakhani suggest, 'it is difficult to believe that the ethnic and visible minority members of parliament (MPs) in the reform caucus "approach the world of politics based on any promotion of their own ancestral origins."'[179] The new, visible minority Reform MPs arrived in Ottawa with strong backgrounds in business. They are more likely to have identified in terms of *class* with the neoliberal economic and financial platforms of the Reform Party, and with an immigration policy that favours 'investor immigrants', and were thus undeterred by the party's 'all-white image'.[180] A lecture hall is no different. Why should a researcher from overseas sense a particular affiliation with students from the same country? Would not this particular scientist feel more closely affiliated to his academic colleagues? During an interview with Anders Persson, he expressed concern about the fact that – according to the report's 'mission' – the analytical difference between class and ethnicity should be explicitly ignored. Did this not affect the conclusions? Yes, he replied. As a founding principle of sympathy and antipathy, multiculturalism evades intellectual predisposition and class, while displaying perfect pitch for roots and skin colour – a community in equal proportion based on appearance and myth. Socialist class struggle is not jeopardised by a sentimentalist right, but by a culturally obsessed multiculturalism.

Diversity at the University may, as I showed above, appear reactionary because we are expected to show sympathy and antipathy by means of the visual flock instinct – the way animals do. But there is more to it. Molefi Asante is one of the more prominent spokespersons for ethnic representation – above all for black people. – and the inherent benefits of child and teacher belonging to the same ethnic group. 'Undeniably', Asante maintains in a sentimental tone, 'segregation was legally and morally wrong'. At the same time, the children 'achieved something in these school in a sense as important as new books, better educated teachers, and better equipped classrooms. The children were culturally centred which made teaching more interesting and intimate'.[181]

In this respect, the report does not lack critical discussion and is aware of exaggerations, 'where the inherent worth of group identities rather than science'[182] has led to a situation in which academic literature that does not 'affirm our culture' or 'support our religion' should be replaced by 'supportive' and 'affirming' teaching materials. *Diversity at the University* takes note of radical forms of multiculturalism, where the majority culture is branded as 'an oppression against minority cultures at the same time as' the minority culture itself 'is ethnocentric and hence a weapon' in a naked power struggle.[183] These critical insights, however, are lost in the general discussion. The report states, 'Role models in teaching are of great value in education.'[184] 'The quality of education', it is claimed, 'depends upon how well the students can recognize themselves in the teacher.'[185]

On a primitive level, a teacher from the same ethnic group as the students may well, as argued by Asante, create a sense of intimacy. But why should we be primitive? What, exactly, is gained if Swedish students are exclusively being taught by blond men and women? *Diversity at the University* does not necessarily express the views of Molefi Asante. But if the price of ethnic representation includes drawbacks (everything comes with a cost), the rationale behind Asante is unavoidable: The teaching situation becomes 'more interesting'. because the teacher is free to approach the material uninhibited by scientific principles. Ethnocentric teaching materials characterised by multicultural 'affirmation' is uncritical to one's own history. Its purpose is to support, cherish, boost, and celebrate the experience of one ethnic group – at the expense, presumably, of the experiences and merits of other groups, and of scientific accuracy. A native, self-mystifying charlatan, and not the wonders of science, has the power to make teaching 'more interesting'. Emblematic anti-intellectualism.

On second thought, the difference between classic imperialism and multicultural affirmation vanishes. Whether cultural affirmation goes under the name of euro-centrism, British jingoism, afrocentrism, or semitocentrism, it will inevitably end in pathetic self-perception, an unscientific view of historical events, obsession with political victories and defeats, submissive and idealising portraits of ancestors and the like. 'Afrocentric teaching material' – argues

Yehudi O. Webster – 'overflows with errors' and 'does not even pretend to offer an unbiased scientific view'. 'History teaching cannot', he continues, 'be about having worship for ancestors drummed into you'.[186] Multicultural celebration of ethnocentrism and imperialist euro-centrism from yesterday are one and the same, since, as noted by C. P. Banner-Haley, the previous one is 'a mythology that is racist, reactionary, mainly therapeutical and racism with a black face'.[187] Whether you hail one culture and reject another or do it the other way around, you are caught in a mental whirlwind about who is to be denigrated and who is to be celebrated; whose culture is deep, majestic, and authentic, and whose is shallow, pathetic, and stolen. A more superficial antagonism than the one between old-school imperialists and today's multiculturalists is not easy to find. Yet, again, I wish to draw attention to Bernhard Crick: 'Do not treat any culture as superior or inferior.' To return to Asante, we must also ask just how much cultural affirmation a modern society can tolerate without disintegrating. Ahmed Ifthikar from the London School of Economics and Political Sciences claims that the reason why Muslim children have bad grades is caused partly by the fact that they read the Koran too much.[188]

Advocates of ethnic pride of a more traditional kind, such as national socialists and fascists, have a passion for a past idyll when signs in bars and on park benches read: 'whites only'. Multiculturalists would not call themselves racists. Still, the ethnic representation in the report is a kind of 'blacks only'. While classic nationalists mock intellectuals and dismiss formal qualifications for the benefit of *Blut und Boden* and the right skin colour, the multiculturalists have a soft spot for indigeneous teachers uncontaminated by Western intellectualism and modernity. They are all pessimists, since they leave no hope for cross-cultural understanding. We can't live together. They shrug their shoulders. In the rhetoric of the French Nouvelle Droite, this is called ethno-pluralism where 'Africans live there and the French live here'. In diversity rhetoric it goes under the name of 'intimacy' and 'cultural centering'. Rumy Hasan argues that multiculturalism is about 'plural monoculturalism', and so the line between a pampered and a calumniated ethno-mystique is increasingly blurred.[189] The classic nationalist and the multiculturalists behind *Diversity at the University* both express conservative views; the radical rightist always acknowledged it, the multiculturalist always denied it.

Based on the fact that identity – in the report – is defined as visual recognition, the question arises: What is the common ground of a physically fit and a physically disabled human being? Once, I had to keep a Riesenschnauzer dog on a tight leash when she tried to attack a disabled young man as he stumbled towards his front door. Animals are naturally inclined to treat weakness and physical deviation with contempt. This is how they preserve their territory. How are we humans supposed to act? Diversity is a good alibi for political violence.

Where does the idea of representation in society come from? It comes from a criticism against a sense of exclusion, going back to the privileges of the upper class of the early 20th century. This particular injustice is the key to the multicultural argument. Class society did not, however, crumble because of multiculturalism. It crumbled because of the idea that a position should be offered to the most able candidate irrespective of background. This is called meritocracy. Less well qualified 'insiders' should not overtake qualified candidates of 'lesser means'. Moreover, these ideas did *not* demand that a given percentage should be assigned to workers, but that the best candidate should get the job. These theories are originally to be found in the writings of the German sociologist Max Weber and his ideas about a modern state apparatus – transparent, meritocratic, and under the rule of law.

These three theories for job recruitment merit a comparison. Upper-class privileges of pre-democratic times and the Weberian state apparatus are clearly distinct. Upper-class privileges and the idea of representation in society are, however, under the surface, very similar. In both cases the meritocratic idea is pushed aside only to be replaced by the 'right of the minority'. I fail to be convinced by the fact that the multicultural minority is perceived as 'good' while the upper-class minority is 'bad'. Hitler also claimed that what he did was good. Moralism belongs to party politics. Representation in society is an attack on modernity and rationality. It is old wine in new bottles. Why is this discussion overlooked in *Diversity at the University*?

So far, the discussion has focused on the assumed benefits of a representational society. But this idea is not uncontroversial. The multicultural attack against class society is much ado about nothing. The optical basis for identification appears inhuman. Ethnic 'intimacy' fuels self-mystification and undermines knowledge. What about the other part of the phrase? 'What about society? 'University's legitimacy in society increases', we are told, by ethnic diversity.[190] But is this really about living up to the desires of an entire society – or even a majority in it? The bulk of advocates behind 'representation in society' are in media, politics, and academia – i.e. within the so-called 'elite'. Meanwhile the feelings towards these values are somewhat cooler among the general population. Why, then, does *Diversity at the University* refer to legitimacy in society when it is merely about the views among a minority, admittedly a powerful one? What if all this advocacy on behalf of ethnic minorities is merely a mirror-image of one's own craving for power – as opposed to the silent majority who no longer can think accurately nor vote properly? This comment unfolds a completely different discussion: How is this majority perceived in *Diversity at the University*? What about worn-out ideas such as 'people' and 'the rule of the majority'? Historically, the majority has treated minorities with ruthlessness. In Sweden, during the 20th century, forced sterilisations were performed on people deemed 'unfit'. But multicultural and postmodernist attitudes against those who *do not* deviate are also problematic. *Diversity at the University* advocates on behalf of talented children from the working classes and their access to the university – indeed an indicator of a society's democratic stamina. Anders Persson maintains that talent is proportionate among classes, and something should be done about this. I could not agree more. But then who are these children of the majority who might not necessarily embrace the idea of representation in society? Voting cattle? White trash proletariat or 'losers in the process of modernisation'? Sweden Democrats? Do multiculturalists really want these groups to engage in university studies?[191]

Back to the main message and the 'society' according to which universities seek legitimacy. In short, we are faced with an alliance between values that not even *Diversity at the University* can properly defend ('Diversity leads to quality'), and a 'society' that has little legitimacy outside a ruling elite; the very elite behind the 'mission' that was put in the hands of the authors of the report in the first place. The university administrator was commissioned to lend support to a view ('diversity') held by few and proven by even fewer, in order to enjoy the appreciation of something most of us seem to disagree with ('society').

The concept of ethnicity is not as innocent as some seem to think. Ethnic belonging, it is claimed, is good while nationalism is bad. But even if ethnic concord, intimacy, and 'a sense of recognition' are being embraced, this sentimentality can easily be charged with a different content. Ethnic cleansing, a concept that gained a notoriety during the Balkan War, is a good case in point. Here, we can see an overlap between cherished ethnicity and contemptible nationalism. In sharp words Sweden is described as on its path towards an 'ethnic division of labour" i.e. reflection of our 'ethnic hierarchy'. It all sounds both humble and adventurous, but in what sense is Sweden of today characterised by ethnic hierarchy? And how come, in a report where ethnicity is painted in rosy colours left, right, and centre, it is suddenly tainted with right-wing extremism? We need to make a choice. Ethnic diversity is either good, or not good. But *Diversity at the University* does not offer a choice. Instead, it seems, it is motivated by emotional conviction. It is not about ideas and their merits and pitfalls, such as whether a multicultural approach is good or not. It is about geography and, on the needle of the ethnic compass, we are indicated by storm. An indigeneous Swede who wishes to be recognised by a light-skinned person is a multicultural comedian. 'Measures must be taken at once' in case an organisation displays more Swedes than allowed for by our 'quota'. The fact that the welfare state, since the time of the early 20th century Social Democrat Ernst Wigforss, rests on a

foundation of professional merits, can be wiped aside with a half-smile. Respect for our social institutions inspired by 20th century social democracy is replaced by soothing self-harassment.
In the eyes of George Orwell, this is 'negative nationalism';[192] a nationalism as self-obsessed, unscientific, and sentimental as any British 'jingoism' and classic nationalism ever were, distinguished only by the fact that 'we' no longer occupy the top rung but rather constitute a mediocre bunch who must refrain from pointing fingers at others before having cleaned in front of our own front door. In its own way, this is a remarkably useful self-obsession, because 'there is always the dirtiest corner in the room'. Regarding 'the other', however, critiques of ethnic homogeneity and identification are being lost in a mist of myths and idealism. Other ethnic groups 'identify' with 'their own kind', and Swedish organisations are 'enriched' by other cultures. The service sector in Dubai is chiefly constituted by foreign labourers living in abysmal conditions. But why bring up 'ethnic division of labour' when you can dine at the foot of *Burj Khalifa* while enjoying water fountains with strings? Orwell, who had a concept for many things, refers to this as 'transferred nationalism', a kind of nationalism barred at home but hailed overseas because it is being legitimised by our sense of liberal postcolonial guilt, as a case of classic psychological compensation.[193] According to Orwell, this is the same nationalism, only not *here* but *over there.* 'I believe this is a little bit why many Swedes are so jealous of immigrant groups', says Mona Sahlin, Social Democrat and previous Prime Minister candidate. 'You have a culture, an identity, a history, something that binds you together. What do we have? We have Midsummer's Eve and ridiculous stuff like that.'[194]

Sahlin's words reflect decades of self-abusive discourse within the Swedish political elite. As a consequence of our own xenophile blinders, Wolfgang Kowalsky claims that the troublesome aspects in exotic cultures are overlooked for the benefit of their beauty and multicultural exoticism. The argumentative logic is this: 'the reason why foreigners are met with such jealousy and hate by the domestic population is because foreigners lead such a tempting alternative way of life.' 'The lack of realism in such a simplistic interpretation',

Kowalsky continues, 'can hardly be rivalled.'[195] Sahlin's statement was moreover commented on by Karen Jespersen, Denmark's former Minister of Integration, 'It's hard for cultural self-denial to be more monstrous and horrifying than this.'[196]

When you side with transferred nationalism, you can be much more partial, vengeful, and tendentious than you would ever dare to be at home, because we lack knowledge about these cultures. 'Transferred nationalism', Orwell claims, 'is a way of receiving salvation without changing your conduct'.[197] This is the reason, I would claim, why *Diversity at the University* can show such a sentimental attitude towards immigrant groups. Additionally, one remains unimpressed by decades of ambitions in the field of integration; by home language education, Swedish for Immigrants, support personnel, migration authorities, ministers of immigration, quotas for immigrants, adjustment guides, special treatment, committees, policies and measures – and *Diversity at the University*. In the report, ethnic diversity oscillates between being a safe haven for a tormented ethnic minority and an expression for right-wing extremism. By implication, therefore, the concept has ceased to exist as *an idea*. Ethnic pride is good and it is bad. The Swedish national romantic poet Verner von Heidenstam is not good, and German traditions are also not good, but Buddha statues are inspirational.[198]

Earlier, we discussed the idea that diversity leads to quality. But the statistical evidence was not clear. Co-existence might be a bad thing. Sometimes it leads to violence. What about all those efforts to reduce the marginalisation of immigrant groups at the university? What can statistical material tell us? In order to minimise the risk of being biased, the only material cited is to be found on the pages of *Diversity at the University*. We are told that the authors of the report, 'developed figures where the ethnic diversity among university staff is being presented'. In relation to the entire Swedish population, 'universities display an over-representation of individuals born abroad, and 10 per cent of those employed at the university have foreign citizenship, while similar figures among the population at large is 5 per cent'.[199] Other statistics cited show a weak correlation between ethnic background and higher education.

On the opening pages of the report, 'the proportion of students with foreign background at the level of university', it is noted, 'is roughly equal to that of the general population'. 'In terms of ethnic recruitment, no figures indicate that individuals with a minority background, considered a group, would be unfavourably treated in the recruitment process of higher education.' The report continues, 'this supports Eriksson and Jonsson's conclusion that immigrant background by and large does not appear to have a negative effect upon the likelihood of engaging in academic studies'.[200] The report can draw these conclusions against the background of other studies – Swedish studies as well as international ones. These studies appear to show that ethnicity as a concept is subordinate to the concept of class, because, 'when individuals with similar social background are compared, the negative effect of ethnicity on education is only marginally negative'.[201] 'The statistical material as well as research about minority groups in higher education', is not 'particularly conclusive,' the report adds.[202]

Material cited in *Diversity at the University* does not lend support to the idea that ethnic minority groups are being marginalised in Swedish higher education. The correlation seems to be close to zero. Regarding university staff, the statistical material even suggests an 'over-representation among those with a foreign background.' And we are told that ethnicity, once you cater for social class, does not say much really. Your class says a lot about your likelihood of engaging in higher studies. Your ethnic background, on the other hand, says very little. Hence, there ought to be a clear line of demarcation between the two. But, as we have already discussed, one of the authors of the report was concerned about the fact that his task did not allow for any distinction between class and ethnicity. Diversity rhetoric seeks legitimacy by acting as a subheading to class. But the result does not mean anything. Thus you might question the scientific basis for *Diversity at the University* and, by implication, the multicultural agenda as such. The university administrators are expected to live up to a 'mantra', which is supposed to respond to 'societal views' according to society's multicultural elite, all of which are ultimately based on statistical material twisting and turning like a worm on a hook.

Research on 'immigrants in the educational system' is not, it is claimed, 'particularly extensive'. Then one would expect cautious conclusions. Why this air of sensation when there is no fact to prove it? If, moreover, diversity is about different life-styles co-habiting in harmony, should not the universities, too, be included? Does it make sense to cherish the principle of diversity when all critiques against this principle are silenced? In case we cannot ask ethnic minorities to reflect the life-style of the majority, why is the university, this fragile and haunted institution, obliged to reflect society at large?

Internationalisation and neoliberalism

What is the relation between diversity, on the one hand, and internationalisation and neoliberalism on the other? In *Diversity at the University*, internationalisation is widely cherished, and the connection to diversity is seen as obvious. In the report, 'international experience (...) or work related to diversity in higher education is emphasised.'[203] A global financial system where borders between nations disappear calls for trans-ethnic skills: 'Multicultural competence is increasingly important in a labour market characterised by a global economy'.[204] Our multicultural institutions of higher learning are warmly approved in the report, and this colourfulness is caused by an extensive exchange of researchers: 'Among university researchers and teachers, there is, as evidenced by the report, a great number of individuals with a foreign background. This ethnic diversity, it seems, is predominantly the result of a successful internationalisation of research'.[205] It is, moreover, important to ensure that 'the multicultural environment of the university is manifest and will be utilised in the process of internationalisation'.[206] Furnished 'with their cultural knowledge and experience, teachers and researchers from other countries (...) are a great asset to the university, and should be seen as a natural part of our strategy of internationalisation at home'.[207]

In the report, internationalisation is seen as progressive and as a natural compliment to diversity. The problem is that diversity – including the culturally relativistic idea of separate ethnic enclaves – is offbeat with globalisation and deregulation. If we can speak at all about a relation between diversity as an ambitious social model and international academic exchange, diversity *prevents* global academic cooperation. Surely universities may engage in emotional exchange of cultural experience. But are universities the proper place for cultural sentimentality?

Spin-doctors of diversity may be well advised to link up with internationalism, academic exchange, and a globalised economy. But the connection is unfounded. Internationalisation is associated with a diehard universalism, standardising and the tearing down of frontiers, while diversity is linked to a sentimental relativism and ethnic homogeneity, with the celebration of the diverging, the local, and the temporal, and with an anti-modernist ambition to dissolve 'totalitarian aspirations'. Diversity has been trivialised beyond recognition, if it signifies nothing but visiting professors. If the report seeks to defend diversity, it should be pursued along the lines of its own premises: identity politics, anti-individualism, and collectivist self-idealisation. It is an injustice to diversity as a poetically appealing idea if it is associated with cool science and boundary free internationalism.

Claiming that diversity is opposed to values vaguely associated with internationalisation and globalisation is only half-true. While diversity in many ways is opposed to internationalisation, it may still be associated with similar ideas. Above all, this refers to tendencies under the banner of neoliberalism. Diversity and neoliberalism often unite in joint projects.

The report brings up a few examples. In spring of 1999, the Swedish Department of Commerce decided to launch a project of 'productive diversity' in business and in the labour market, entitled Mångfaldsprojektet ('The diversity project'). The project was to result in a 'national program for productive diversity in trade and industry' where 'ethnic diversity in higher education (is playing) an important role' – a good example of a fusion between diversity and market principles.[208] Under 'The University is assigned a central role in the development of society', multicultural rhetoric is combined with neoliberal maximisation of profit: 'Various forms of distance, among them those of a cultural nature, must be overcome'. This 'should be done without losing what is culturally distinct at a university, and in particular its exciting and creative mix of knowledge, critical thinking and usefulness'.[209] Higher learning's specific nature is, thus, 'cultural'. Hence, the university becomes part of the ideology of diversity – and cultural distinction is created by declaring the border between intellectual autonomy and costumer adjustment invalid. What is to 'be retained' is no longer intellectualism but culturalism: colours, ceremonies, events, ethnic mixture, religious pluralism, and so on. The university is not characterised by intellectual life, but by the forms and rituals of this intellectual life – no longer by the discreet and truly original, but by the highly coloured, opportunistic, conformist, and truly trivial. Higher education is being reshaped with culturalism as an anvil and neoliberalism as a hammer.

This intellectual recklessness, an obsession with culture in its most banal sense, and the disposition to refer to all of it as 'exciting' and 'creative' characterises both diversity and neo-liberalism. The rhetoric about cultural recognition – i.e. to retain one's culture intact – suits anyone who wishes to stay clear of economic recognition. Similarly, cultural recognition comes in handy for those who seek to obstruct intellectual recognition and independence. Pluralism and variety have been deprived of all content.

Cultural distance, we are told, most be 'overcome'. This declaration can be critically assessed from two perspectives. If we, first, assume that cultural differences are decisive and that all other qualities are coloured by them, the question arises: Why must differences be overcome? Whether differences and conflicts are overcome or sharpened is not an emotional issue but a practical one, decided by circumstances. With respect to intellectual 'distance', conflicts cannot be overcome unless the very essence of a university ceases to exist. The idea of a university is that conflicts and diverging views are accepted and perhaps underscored, all of which, it is worth emphasising, is done in a civilised manner. The idea that differences must be 'overcome' assumes that different views inevitably spark hatred, and therefore must be overcome through administrative means – at heart a conservative idea whereby conflicts among the populace are deemed destructive and to be resolved by a bureaucratic elite. The result is not diversity but mental discipline. At this point, we are witnessing yet another link between diversity and neoliberalism; namely a bourgeois, neurotic, and authoritarian wish to dissolve the intellectual conflict and replace it with anything that is 'good' and that 'works'.

When differences are overcome by administrative means, this will lead to hegemonic power that – and this is the very problem with hegemony – will gradually become void, self-centred, emotionally exalted, and full of hate. This is an appropriate description of hegemonic multiculturalism in Sweden. Generally, diversity's academic advocates in this country have only a limited knowledge about the intricacies involved, and critiques are as a matter of routine, met with a blend of therapy and emotional outbursts: "I am against multiculturalism'. 'But, please, how can you say such a thing?' This is the harsh reality behind the rhetoric of 'overcoming differences': hegemony without harmony – hatred without open conflict. The Russian Revolution, the socialist Victor Serge describes in *Memoirs of a Revolutionary*, created a hegemonic feeling of having access to the absolute truth. Any deviation, as a result, was subject to contempt. Instead, Serge proposes, we should do it the other way around – try to combine strong convictions and the uncompromising attitude that goes with it 'with respect for the individual behind the enemy; in short: war without hatred'.[210]

Here, too, diversity and neoliberalism are combined: while the former exerts hegemonic power in the realm of culture and intellectual life, the latter has hegemonic power in economic matters. In both cases we are taught what is 'good' and 'right', instead of a discussion *about* good and bad and right and wrong and its nuances. While diversity is perceived as post-cultural among the new left-wingers, neoliberalism is seen as post-ideological by its protagonists. Critiques against diversity are deemed as right-wing extremism, while critiques against neoliberalism are a call for worker's riots. Why, besides, should 'cultural differences' cease to exist merely because these words are printed in a Social Democratic government report? Would we not, then, exaggerate the impact of a government paper, and underestimate our values' depth and authenticity?

But the rhetoric of cultural distance may also be criticised from the opposite end. This idea rests on the assumption that it constitutes a real problem in higher education. But this is not so. When an international group of researchers gets together, we do not bother about cultural differences. We try to get some work done.

Background, roots, all those things are irrelevant. They have been ever since background, origin, contacts, and heritage slowly were replaced by formal qualifications in the early 20th century. While diversity tries to replace merit with culture, neoliberalism tries to supplant it with class society. They both oppose modernity.

Diversity's current position in society, I argue above, can be compared to the role of Marxism in the early 1970s. In both cases, it is about a practically hegemonic discourse. Still, there are differences. The Marxist critique against capitalism was intellectual by nature. Another difference has to do with the fact that Marxism, despite its dominant role at the university, never lost its political/subjective ambition. It never became bureaucratic and canting, or let alone, sought to fuse with trade and business. At the time, there were, for instance, no 'class managers' or 'conflict officers'. In contrast, 'Diversity Managers' and 'Diversity Officers' have quickly gained a wide footing – a good case of a successful alliance between multiculturalism and neoliberalism.[211] One of these Diversity Managers did, for instance, participate in the drafting of the report.[212] The purpose of these combined concepts is to achieve legitimacy through bureaucratisation and institutionalisation. Another disparity is the fact that Marxists never saw their ideas on par with environmental issues at work. Here, too, they are surpassed by diversity. The Safety Committee at the Faculty of Odontology, Malmö University College is entitled 'The Committee for work environment, gender equality, and diversity'. The way in which the ideology of diversity is being bureaucratised shows another link to neoliberalism – namely 'Death of ideologies' where the fruitless ideological struggle of factions has left the stage for the benefit of the managers of the state, aiming for 'good' and 'constructive' solutions that 'make a difference!' Let us not choose bad solutions, but good ones, multiculturalists and neoliberals say. As opposed to Marxists, Diversity Managers are perfectly at ease among neoliberal spin-doctors and lobbyists. Even if 'Diversity Manager' might sound reassuring, it merely shows us that multiculturalism has greater ambitions than Marxism ever had, and has sunk even deeper into the realm of our subconscious.

While being extremely versatile in its critique, it should be noted that universities' recurring liaison with the world of commerce is exempt from critique by the multiculturalists – possibly because trade and business back multiculturalism. In a situation where diversity discourse is hegemonic and a safe platform for a career – 'in America this is a billion-dollar industry' – it makes sense for business people to link up with diversity.[213] Diversity consultants are probably as pragmatic as the authors of *Diversity at the University* seem to be. Diversity might not be true, but it gives you an income. If politicians change their views when they find a new job, why, then, are multiculturalists obliged to be idealists?

The Marxist philosopher Slavoj Žižek sees the problem from the other end. It is less about neoliberal opportunists profiting on hegemonic multiculturalism, than diversity being exploited by neoliberalism. When everybody silently has accepted that neo-liberalism 'is here to stay – critical energy has found a substitute outlet in fighting for cultural differences which leave the basic homogeneity of the capitalist world-system intact'. Therefore, Žižek continues, 'we are fighting our politically correct battles for the rights of ethnic minorities, of gays and lesbians, different life-styles and so on, while capitalism pursues its triumphant march. At present, post-modern theory 'in the guise of "cultural studies", is doing the ultimate service to the unrestrained development of capitalism by actively participating in the ideological effort to render its massive presence invisible: in a typical postmodern "cultural criticism", the very mention of capitalism as world system tends to give rise to the accusation of "essentialism", "fundamentalism" and other crimes.'[214]

He continues that multiculturalism constitutes the ideal form of ideology of this global capitalism, an 'attitude which, from a kind of empty global position, treats *each* local culture the way the colonizer treats colonized people – as "natives" whose mores are to be carefully studied and "respected"'. The relationship between classic imperialist colonialism and global capitalist self-colonisation 'is exactly the same as the relationship between Western cultural imperialism and multiculturalism'. Just like global capitalism involves the puzzling fact of colonising without the colonising Nation-State, 'multi-culturalism involves patronizing euro-centrist distance and/or respect for local cultures without roots in one's own particular culture'. Therefore, Žižek carries on, multiculturalism is a disavowed, inverted, self-referential form of racism, a 'racism with a distance' – it 'respects' the Other's identity, conceiving the Other as a self-enclosed 'authentic' community towards which the multiculturalist maintains a distance rendered possible by his or her privileged universal position. 'Multiculturalism is a racism which empties its own position of all positive content (...) but nonetheless retains this position as the privileged empty point of universality from which one is able to appreciate (and depreciate) properly other particular cultures.' The multiculturalists own 'superiority' is revealed precisely by their 'respect for the Other's specificity'.[215] Our arrogance is indicated by our humbleness only, and our power so overwhelming, we do not even raise our voice.

In the eyes of the Marxist Perry Anderson, diversity is also a tool in the hands of neoliberal forces. He takes as his starting point the fact that these forces – he refers to the EU – see all class struggle as an anathema and threat against elite privileges. At this point, ethnic conflict comes in handy. What actually has happened, he says, is that 'ethno-religious tensions have displaced class antagonisms'. Instead of uniting against capital and state, domestic workers attack *other* workers: 'the poor revile the poor'. The fact that the working class and immigrants often have common interests has also been carefully obscured by the multiculturalists, always keen to separate ethnic groups from one another.[216] Again, it seems, multiculturalists have played into the hands of neoliberalism. The reason, according to Anderson, as to why the working class has drifted to the right is not ideology ('They have become racists!'), but a change 'in its relative position in society'. At the bottom rung of the social ladder, where they used to be, we now find the immigrant. At the same time, the situation of workers 'is weaker and more insecure than before, in societies where industry is no longer much honoured and inequality has been steadily rising'.[217] Multiculturalism has furnished the neoliberal elite with a common power tool – divide and rule. The radicalism of this right-wing symbiosis makes is difficult to distinguish liberal from Marxist critiques. To an economic elite without scruples, common demands from marginalised groups, writes Brian Barry, is 'a nightmare'. The best bet is to incite them against each other. 'Diverging attention away from shared disadvantages such as unemployment, poverty, low-quality housing and inadequate public services is an obvious long term anti-egalitarian objective'.[218]

Perry Anderson remains no less unconvinced whether the EU – according to him the embodiment of radical market solutions – really can contribute to integration and social peace. Perhaps the purpose is to *oppose* integration, undermine the welfare state, and dissolve social trust – all in order to pave the way for neoliberal social transformations.[219] Žižek also fails to believe that the working class has made a right-wing turn because they must be racists. Rather, the working class has been abandoned by the multicultural elite: 'While multicultural tolerance becomes the motto of the new and privileged "symbolic" classes, the far Right seeks to address and to mobilize whatever remains of the mainstream "working class" in our Western societies.' In this one-sided spectrum, he continues: 'political differences are more and more reduced to merely cultural attitudes: multicultural/sexual (etc.) "openness" versus traditional/natural (etc.) "family values"'. The left has endured a most arduous castling, 'a social democracy purged of its minimal subversive sting, extinguishing even the faintest memory of anti-capitalism and class struggle'.[220]

The multiculturalists say that the right-wing parties do not allow people of other skin colour into their ranks. They only allow for members of their 'own' skin complexion. While this is indeed true regarding ultra-right wing parties, such as Svenskarnas Parti and the Greek Golden Dawn, it is not true for most parties perceived to be right-wing populists or worse. In fact, many of them appear versatile in classic working-class rhetoric where ethnic demarcation lines do not count. Marine Le Pen, leader of the French *Front National*, claims that French workers of all races will suffer form the ever-increasing influx of Romanians and Poles. In case Le Pen's statement reveals a bigger picture, we may witness one of the multiculturalists' biggest failures – handing over the entire idea of class antagonism and solidarity to the right-wingers.[221]

Apart from the above-cited documents and the analyses of Žižek and Anderson, the connection between diversity and neoliberalism can be supported by a few additional arguments. Neoliberals say: you do not need institutions. You are strong and independent. The state says it speaks on your behalf, but in fact it speaks on behalf of others. Make yourself heard through pressure groups and lobbying. Multiculturalists say: cut loose from the oppression by the majority and the state. Seek the company of your own kind. Try to have influence upon the state and on institutions – but not through the state, but via group representation. Your group speaks on your behalf; the state does not.

See through the liberal illusion of one person-one vote, we are told by the protagonists of diversity. The parliament acts on behalf of the majority and the vengeful crowds. The parliament is corrupt and reactionary. The parliament, the neo-liberals claim, is political and hence bound hand-and-foot. The parliament is corrupt and reactionary. Neoliberals turn to those who are, or wish to be, different and special: part of a distinct minority with the right to ask for favours *out of the ordinary* due to their wealth and their power. Diversity sides with a minority that seeks recognition and special treatment due to their 'powerlessness'. While neoliberals are unaffected by it, this streak of elitism and snobbism might make the multiculturalist slightly uneasy. Society's so-called elite has a soft spot for diversity because it attacks the majority and fulfils their craving for excitement and desire to feel extraordinary, but also because the discourse of diversity has a reputation for being progressive and safely self-humiliating.

'Good for you! the neo-liberal exclaims when someone makes a profit under the nose of all the others. Good for you, but bad for us. Lucky you! the multiculturalist greets when an ethnic group acquires special favours. Good for you, not so good for the others.

Both invite for a feast on the cadaver of the common. With joint efforts, the neo-liberal and the multiculturalist dissolve social trust to have it replaced by clamorous egotism. They both seek appreciation for their greed, and they sing the swan song for society *as we know it.* Touched by postmodernity, they have been mesmerised by anti-utopianism and the belief that any excess of decadence, group egotism and minority arrogance, is better than a pinch of transcultural, cross-ethnic, inter-religious solidarity. If solidarity, irrespective of who you are, constituted a leap forward in human thinking, diversity and neoliberalism display a concomitant leap backwards; the former because it is merely pseudo-radical, under the surface overflowing with myths, ethno-pessimism, and 'culturalism and misanthropy', the latter because we have seen it all before – day labourers, slave contracts, and so on – until democracy finally, during early 20th century, came out victorious.[222]

Threatened by neoliberal anarchy such as the erosion of wages, business migration and supra-national agreements above and beyond the reach of national legislation, Social Democracy has become sentimental and conservative while trying to save the rubble of the welfare state project. All that is solid melts into air by the revolutionary onslaught from the right. Under the shadow of impending neoliberal financial meltdown and dissolution of all norms, classic social democracy can hope for nothing but the status quo. Diversity, the report claims, 'opens up multifaceted ways of getting to grips with the work task'.[223] An ethnic minority fails unless it sets about a job in diversified ways. Sticking to the tradition of the Swedish public officer is not equivalent to transparency, the rule of law and all-encompassing comradeship, but tantamount to white supremacy and neglecting individuals from overseas. Diversity liberates us from the law and from the oppression of the slow and hesitating majority. The floodgates of neoliberalism are opened by diversity.

Then again, if neo-liberalism threatens revolution while classic Social Democracy tries to stand up for modernity, what kind of revolution is it really about? It is, Pierre Bourdieu insists, a 'conservative revolution'. The modern project is being dismantled and a system from the past is reinstalled. Through neo-liberalism, 'under the pretence of a modern and fashionable message, we are witnessing the return of the most cherished ideas of yesterday's employers.' Any *conservative revolution*, for instance Reagan's Presidency in the United States and the Nazi era, is characterised by 'an effort to depict restorations as revolutions'.[224] 'Neo-liberal utopia', Bourdieu maintains, is an 'infernal machine' from the past, and the result 'a Darwinian business spirit, based on insecurity, human suffering and stress'.[225] In its aversion against modernity – against citizenship, majority principle, and rule of law, neoliberalism makes common cause with diversity.

The modern idea is essentially the idea of a common and secular society; we are united more than separated, and ethnicity is being replaced by the nation as a 'development project based on citizenship'.[226] Equality in education enables variation based on merit. Irrespective of background, everybody should enjoy the same basic knowledge in a wide range of disciplines – paving the way for freedom of choice at a later stage. Group myths are counteracted by a modern educational system based on secular principles, creating solidarity with those who are different. A public school owned by the state runs counter to injustice and is part of a social glue, without which, society will fall asunder.

What do neo-liberals and multiculturalists say about this? The state stifles freedom of choice. Without deregulation and free competition we will all be grey and uniform. Private schools – allowing for the free expression of all opinions and views, be it aesthetic, religious, or cultural – are therefore advocated. Let a thousand flowers blossom. Without freedom of choice at school, the multiculturalist say, the authenticity among ethnic, religious, and cultural minorities is jeopardised. Private schools are therefore vital in a tolerant society, where a multitude of viewpoints can freely interact with each other in concord in a free and open context. Let a thousand flowers blossom. The modernists say: the unitary school levels out inequalities between groups. Autonomy is provided by the state. The unitary school suppresses minorities, multiculturalists and neoliberals insist. Autonomy is endangered by the state. Without a secular unitary school, the former claim, religious pluralism cannot be guaranteed. Religious minorities are repressed in the unitary school, multiculturalists and neoliberals claim. The unitary school, says the modernist, enables us to act united as citizens in a political community. The private school makes it possible for ethnic groups to act in concord in a cultural community, says the multiculturalist, while the private school, in the eyes of the neoliberal, offers an opportunity to launch neoliberal views, further undermining the common political project. The fact that the silent majority tends to defend the unitary school fails to convince those who only have eyes for minorities.[227] The one type of diversity lost in the multicultural and neoliberal equation is *political diversity*; since political pluralism questions the idea of the disfavoured unified ethnic minority according to the former, and because politics, as such, is perceived as repressive and passé according to the latter.

It would be unfair to portray *Diversity at the University* as out-and-out biased. The report brings to attention Elisabeth Gerle. She maintains that we, as convinced modernists, must not fall into the trap of 'ethnic racism', and group identity, and a 'one-sided focus on the different and the exotic makes it harder for us to observe commonalities'.[228] The Norwegian anthropologist Thomas Hylland Eriksen engages in a similar discussion based on the term 'cultural terrorism'. At the same time, he adds, our ambitions to integrate 'the Other' may easily appear patronising.[229]

Recently, I happened to see a TV commercial, in which individuals from a distant land – I believe it was Thailand – were performing advanced dance rituals, swinging rods, and the like. The speed of the images was very high. I sensed that we were almost back to the era of motionless pictures, as the impression of breakneck pace was due to constantly new snaps of imagery. It was all very colourful and all very superficial. Whatever it was about, it was not about Thailand. It struck me, though, as I was watching these vivid images flashing by, that they reminded me of the ways in which exotic ethnic minorities are being portrayed by multiculturalists. Watching the speed and the carnival of disconnected images, and the lack of any scent or real life beyond the glossy surface, it was as if the dead and yet superficially enticing imagery of diversity had suddenly come to life right in front of me. I realised why these stereotypical and lifeless depictions of far-off lands were so familiar. They were already ubiquitous – in the form of colourful TV-commercials. I understood why I was rarely caught by that kind of cultural enthusiasm – I felt it was a smile hinting at your wallet. Multiculturalists are singularly focused on the exterior; our bodies, and our skin colour, hairstyle, clothes, jaw bone, the shape of the skull – and the world of commercialism is obsessed with the same things. Diversity is the academic version of make-up – L'Oréal with a footnote. In the stereotypical advertisements for exotic cultures, filled with dancing, singing and laughing, with rods and sticks in all colours imaginable thrown about, at this point of intense fascination for seductive form and superficial aesthetics, multiculturalism blends with ultra-commercialism. The entire idea of pluralism and diversity, richness, and perhaps the very notion of wealth, has been hijacked by multiculturalists and neoliberals; an alliance between an absolutely confused left, and an absolutely determined right.

By nature, neo-liberalism is non-intellectual and does not value education for its own sake. Instead, it is all about consumer interest: the interest of the government, the interest of the state, the interest of business, the interest of *somebody else.* In the discourse of diversity, integration of ethnic minorities into Swedish society is said to be of prime importance, and so an education leading to a job gets the upper hand compared to studies for its their sake. This trend is further amplified by Sweden's high taxes and welfare state, attracting poorly educated immigrants with safe and sound employment and social assistance in sight.

Multiculturalists, too, focus on the customer interest and are rather dismissive of education as an inherent intellectual endeavour – partly because, they believe, excessive knowledge is patronizing. This tendency towards anti-intellectualism and primitivism is strengthened by diversity's flair for optical variation and suspicion that its hegemony will be jeopardised by a variation of political and philosophical ideas cutting through and inevitably dissolving the ethnic group. Plenty of examples of a fusion between diversity and industry can be found on the websites of Swedish universities. Neoliberals oppose egalitarianism and propose instead a hierarchical society. Diversity rests on group mystification, anti-individualism and representation based on 'historical roots' – leading to ethno-collectivist self-haughtiness and a hierarchical society.

Not long ago, the left was all about equality: equal rights, equal pay, equal treatment, and equality before the law. Then, something happened: equality was replaced by dissimilarity. Now the right to be different must be respected; and the more different, the better, the richer and the more emancipated and 'diverse'. What is more, differences have turned into hierarchy; homosexuality topping everyday heterosexuality, ethnic minority becoming more exciting than insipid majority, and exotic religiosity superior to diluted Christianity.[230]

Diversity at the University adheres fully to this pattern. First, the welfare state and its economic redistribution, high taxes, and equality, is criticised by neoliberalism. Instead of this, 'individual independence' is proposed – in others words inequality. Second, diversity and neoliberalism unite in a critique against equality and in their defence of inequality. Cultural difference, it should be admitted, is different from economic difference, but neoliberals are tempted by the opportunities in hegemonic multiculturalism. The advocates of diversity are silent about their ideals (if any) when approached by the tailored suits of trade and industry. Political power merges with financial power.

Third, the idea of cultural diversity constitutes an irresistable temptation for neoliberals because, instead of addressing pressing issues of economic backwardness and concomitant redistributions, it solely demands that the world should be left, as it were, intact. All required by neoliberals is passive fascination with the exotic spectacle that might, in fact, turn out to be a civil war. In a poignant phrase, Eriksen and Stjernfelt refer to this as 'gentrification of backwardness'.[231]

'They are neither below us nor above us!' During breakfast, a friend makes a comment about our Hanoi helpers – nanny, cleaner, and evening nanny. 'They are just different!' I receive an invitation to the multicultural skies of post-conflict where the gap between a U.N. salary and that of a Vietnamese servant is obscured by cultural diversity. Old leftist rhetoric of conflict has been replaced by multicultural intimacy – not, however, because we are similar but because we are different. This is not about classic conservative concord where social cleavages are trumped by national unity, but about the conservatism of diversity where our conscience is cleared – not by a sense of understanding but by the spell of cultural diversity. 'While multicultural tolerance becomes the motto of the new and privileged "symbolic" classes', Slavoj Žižek writes, 'political differences are more and more reduced to merely cultural attitudes'.[232]

Thus, neoliberals can justify their ideology. All they are required to do is agree with multicultural discretion towards overseas cultures. Addressing our freedom and others' troubles is no longer a call for social change, but a sign of intolerance and racism. The anguish is never about social injustice on the scene, but always about us being caught in hierarchies of class instead of embracing the world's cultural rainbow of pleasure and pain. In case Friedrich Engels' *The Condition of the Working-class in England in 1844* would be subject to today's diversity scheme, he would have been held responsible for class-racism, and subsequently Engels would have appointed the mine owner – the most radical exponent for the mining culture of the 19th century – as community leader for the miners.[233]

In *The Road to Wigan Pier*, George Orwell describes the ways in which the British upper class tried to overcome class differences:

> Perhaps this class-breaking business isn't so simple as it looked! On the contrary, it is a wild ride into the darkness, and it may be that at the end of it the smile will be on the face of the tiger. With loving though slightly patronizing smiles we set out to greet out proletarian brothers, and behold! Our proletarian brothers – in so far as we understand them – are not asking for our greetings, they are asking us to commit suicide. When the bourgeoisie see it in *that* form they take to flight, and if his flight is rapid enough it may carry him to Fascism.[234]

Today, working class idealisation has been replaced by idealisation of foreign cultures. In both cases, it is mainly about a romantic view based on ignorance and emotions because stereotypes – in either way – rule out first-hand knowledge. 'I know', Orwell writes in *The Road to Wigan Pier*, 'enough of the British working class not to idealize it'.[235] It is no less difficult to idealise for instance Indonesia, Ethiopia, or Vietnam for anybody who has lived in these countries. Our ethnic comrades may not show curiosity in case we confront them with our stifled metaphysics and attacks against the nuclear family. Perhaps they would like us to disappear. Faced with this reaction, the multiculturalist will be both surprised and disappointed, and his disillusionment may find a cure in Fascism.

When the Austria Freedom Party under Jörg Haider formed a government coalition with the Austrian People's Party in 2000, the EU applied sanctions against the country. The following citation appeared in *Austria under "EU-quarantine"* (Österreich unter "EU-Quarantäne") – a 560-page key document containing, as it seems, all criticism against 'the government coalition between the ÖVP and the FPÖ': 'Knowing that the party leader of the FPÖ and Head of Carinthia, since May 1999 is member of the government', we 'condemn all denigrating and anti-European utterances, as has been done by the FPÖ and its spokesperson'.[236] Any 'anti-European' statement is associated with right-wing extremism. *All* critique against the EU is 'condemned'. Peter Hervik, well-known Danish diversity proponent, analyses Denmark's somewhat cool attitude towards the EU. We are, he claims, witnessing 'a resistance against "the foreign" outside Denmark, which has changed into a resistance against foreigners in Denmark.'[237] Critique against the EU fuses with racism.

To the EU, the welfare state is a monster with feet of clay. In the eyes of the multiculturalist, the welfare state is by guilt by association linked to nationalism, racism, and by implication national socialism. The idea of the nation is outdated and you cannot trust the people. Allegations of right-wing extremism can only be averted by siding with elitism of any kind, including right-wing extremism. Eager to shine with anti-racism, the multiculturalist runs right into the arms of global capitalism. Multiculturalism is neoliberal in case all critique against the EU is deemed as xenophobic.

All these parallels between neoliberalism and diversity are made from a critical point of view. Multiculturalists refrain from addressing similarities because they oppose neoliberalism. Neo-liberals, however, see it differently. A good example is Friedrich Hayek's 'Catallax' – an ideal society as developed in his *Law, Legislation and Liberty*.[238] In this utopian image, Jens Sörensen maintains, there is no common purpose. Citing Hayek, this is a society 'incompatible with "solidarity"',[239] where 'the only ties holding Big Society together are purely "economic"'.[240] In order to launch a Catallax, a pluralistic (i.e. multicultural) model must be instigated where solidarity is weaker than in a national context. Why is that so? Because, within the framework of a nation, the people are accustomed to limit the scope of the free market for the benefit of social security systems. The deadly enemies of the Catallax, Sörensen concludes, are therefore ideologies leading to solidarity – in particular socialism and nationalism.[241] Suddenly everything is turned upside down: the welfare state is ruined by multiculturalism and solidarity is enabled by nationalism.

Conclusively, this discussion about parallels between neoliberalism and diversity will ask: What is the nature of the values defended by a good neoliberal? 'It is interesting to consider', Jonathan Friedman argues, 'the inversion of perspectives in which a formerly nationalist elite who may have seen "the people" as a motley foreign mixture, today identifies itself as hybrid/multicultural, and views "the people" as dangerously purist.'[242]

They smile generously at those who still value their home country, culture, and history. These 'champagne liberals' are part of an economically independent global elite, making a virtue of their privileged rootlessness and ephemeral existence. Quality time is assigned to dancing dervishes and exotic art, and the children speak three languages but not their mother tongue. Conversations at the international postings are frivolous – 'you simply have to visit Nepal!' – because it is unlikely that one will ever meet again, which, in turn, demonstrates one's soothing homelessness. This form of existence is practically unthinkable without multiculturalism as an overarching ideology.

Diversity or racism – is it that simple?

In the previous chapter, diversity was connected to neoliberalism, and the report's link between diversity and internationalism was put into question. We now turn to the issue of diversity and racism. *Diversity at the University* presents among others the following view: Multiculturalism fights racism and diversity is everything racism is not. Anti-racism is the flagship of diversity.

'Despite committed efforts to spread diversity, tensions between different groups (...) have increased, resulting in xenophobia, "images of us-and-them" and racism.'[243] According to the report, 'various processes has resulted in the population being differentiated ethnically', which moreover, 'has to do with different group identities, discrimination, xenophobia and segregation'.[244] The background to the 'issue of diversity' was in particular 'the immigrants' situation in the early 1990s. It was strongly characterised by racism, xenophobia, discrimination, and marginalisation'.[245] 'The report continues that the situation of numerous immigrants in Sweden is still characterised by 'segregation and marginalisation'.[246] In order to try to put a stop to these tendencies, ideological and normative multiculturalism is being proposed in the social democratic government report. We are told that normative diversity 'is about creating a society which not only is multicultural but also functions in a multicultural manner. This means that diversity is being cherished and xenophobia is counteracted and replaced by increased cultural understanding.'[247] Consequently, increased tension between groups has taken place *despite* zealous efforts to foster diversity and multiculturalism.[248] Successful anti-racism requires that these efforts be intensified.

What does racism mean? The report makes use of a broad definition. Racism, in brief, is tantamount to having negative or 'hostile' attitudes towards strangers. It is therefore difficult to distinguish between general critiques against strangers and racism in the Fascist sense. There is the risk that the concept is watered down and the fundamental nature of the idea goes missing. I sometimes hear people saying that we must also include borderline cases due to the radical nature of racism. I disagree. This principle should be reserved for commonplace phenomena only, and racism is not commonplace. Racism – and along with it Nazism and fascism – illustrates the ground zero of politics. Instead of recklessly throwing them about, we should make use of these concepts sparingly.

This leads to the question: Does diversity prevent right-wing extremism? The answer is: It is not clear. When Jimmie Åkesson – the leader of Sverigedemokraterna – is branded a 'racist', he is not negatively painted. Instead, the net psychological effect is that racists are whitewashed. The report seeks to counter racism. But why not make use of some political/psychological tactics? Mere moralism and emotionalism trivialises the debate, and nobody likes a trivial debate more than populists and racists. When multiculturalists are 'intensifying' their anti-racist activity, they are not trying to understand racism better in order to sharpen their analysis. It merely means that their *emotional rhetoric* is being intensified. The tone of the argument becomes duller and wide sections of a politically untrained electorate is being radicalised. 'Am I a racist, when I want our children to speak Swedish? Next time, I'll vote for Sverigedemokraterna!' Are we no longer allowed to read Tintin because it is 'imperialist'? Are we supposed to celebrate the end of the school year in a 'non-religious' location for fear of abusing minorities? Well, I can still vote!' As a result, racism is not countered by diversity but boosted by it. The multicultural left does not listen to reason when right-wingers raise their voices. Why, then, should aggressive rhetoric from the other end of the spectrum have an impact? Political stereotypes only cause polarisation. By claiming to have sole access to truth, multiculturalists maintain that right-wing extreme views are caused by misunderstanding and may be cured with increased information. Right-wing extreme views are as internally consistent as any other political point of view. Those on the multicultural left do not understand the severity of the situation, and they do not understand what politics are essentially about. For once, the adherents of diversity should pull the relativist card, and, for once, they choose not to. The future looks grim if all we have to do is shout people down. It would of course be a nightmare if the multiculturalists had to handle the resistance in a potential right-wing extreme siege-of-power.

The question whether the discourse of diversity opposes or paves the way for right-wing extreme tendencies deserves somewhat more attention. A few years ago Jean Marie Le Pen – the then leader of the *Front National* – announced that he felt closer to his daughters than to his cousins, and closer to his cousins than to his neighbours, and closer to them than to other Frenchmen and so on. The statement was instantly coined 'Le Pens infamous concentric circle', and the idea was racist or worse. In fact, it is a platitude. Holding your child above everything else is not racist but human. Why, then, does Le Pen say it? Because he wants people to vote for him.

Provocations are part of any anti-establishment party. To the notorious outsider, political harassment is both natural and risk-free. Hans-Georg Betz describes these right-wing strategies as 'fairly banal, yet effective, above all because (the European) political elite has dutifully played its part and fallen into the various traps (right-wing populists) set for them – to the amusement of (the general) public'.[249] According to Max Riedlsperger, it is 'important not to yield to simplified allegations and "typical leftist hyperbole" because a part of Haider's intentions are precisely to provoke a moralistic overreaction from the opposite camp'.[250] What happens in brief is this: the right-wing populist finds moral values close to the heart of the general public that are initially presented to the public in a highly moralistic fashion aimed at splitting the audience. A certain appreciation arises. Then, as expected, the left responds with moral frenzy, signalling the start of the next phase. This consists of the second, triumphant speech to the Austrian audience, whereby they are told that they are seen as 'fascists', 'racists' or 'a disgrace' by the high-and-mighty. Only now, their tactics will gain momentum by means of a second – and decisive – increase of votes. Indeed, as noted by Wolfgang Kowalsky, the far right often simply counts on this 'anti-fascist reflex', whereby the leftist critics fight against imagined enemies of the past.[251] Max Riedlsperger refers to this mechanism as 'the back-fire effect of the charges of right-extremism'.[252] On a silver plate, right-wing populists are handed one trivial human trait after another: love of your country, cherish your culture and your traditions, or be willing to die for your children but perhaps not for anybody else. Extremism is best fought if we separate it from normality and marginalise it. We do not fight extremism if we marginalise ourselves and dissolve the border between extremism and normality. There is a virtual jungle of nuances to the right of the political mainstream: traditionalism, conservatism, nationalism, patriotism and Catholicism, to name but a few. A Social Democrat and a Stalinist are two different things, and a Swede must also be allowed to celebrate her national holiday without standing in the pillory. Right-wing populists need no friends with enemies such as the multiculturalists.

In case diversity's tactics and methods against others may be put in question, what about its own stance? Is it always anti-racist? In practical terms, as noted above, racism means having negative or 'hostile' emotions towards strangers which, leads to the phrase 'xenophobia'. How is this term defined in the literature? According to the Swedish National Encyclopaedia, it is generally identical to racism. Therefore, only a racist has negative emotions towards strangers. There is no room for antipathy against the unknown that is not simultaneously politically extreme. This definition is widely held not only in diversity discourse, but also in society at large. Politicians, journalists, and academics stand up against xenophobia. Being xenophobic is a bad thing. You do not want to be a xenophobic.

The term will be studied from two distinct perspectives. First, xenophobia will be scrutinised by means of a domestic mirror image. Second, the term will be assessed from a radical conservative point of view.

Discussions about xenophobia are often marred by moralism. Therefore, I will suggest the term 'oikophilia' (love of the familiar) – an apt mirror image from private life. Oikophilia is similar to xenophobia, the result of mental distortions with the sole difference that, here, what is to be countered is not hostility but trust. While you can trust the stranger you cannot trust someone close. Distrust of the family was always part of left-wing extremism, and so, xenophobia is, by implication, tied to left-wing extremism. During the age of Stalinism, family members infamously turned each other in because, they had come to understand, the family was a treacherous institution. Your family was your foe and you could only be saved by the unknown and the abstract visions of the political commissary. As a result, socialist utopia was strengthened.

Claiming a principled innocence of strangers is a dark and totalitarian mirror image of an equally principled lack of trust for your friends and your family. Gudrun Schyman – the former party leader of *Vänsterpartiet* (the Swedish left-wing party) is one among those who have criticised the nuclear family. She and her family were having breakfast in Simrishamn, in southern Sweden. Lasse Westman, her then husband, remembers. 'Suddenly, she said: 'I have come up with a new political slogan: Death to the nuclear family!"' 'Do you believe it yourself?' Westman replied.[253] Still, the slogan was only moderately successful. Therefore, the unknown is being embraced as a kind of tactical regrouping and 'extreme-left light'. To cherish, support, and embrace is also, in our neoliberal day and age, more politically fashionable. At this point, the discourse of diversity has a tendency towards racism for two reasons. First, friends and family are subject to the same baseless allegation as 'the Other' had to endure during the heydays of European imperialism. Second, everything unknown is, according to the multiculturalists, lost in a patronising image of the merry savage, revealing that they know very little but feel all the more.

Within radical conservatism, xenophobia is not the problem, but the solution. According to this ideology, the family is always right, and you should always distrust and show contempt for the unknown. Extreme-right parties in the former Eastern Europe say: 'Why is he your enemy? Because he is a stranger!' In its relentless effort to romanticise the other and implicit scorn of friend and family, diversity offers a negation to radical conservatism, fascism, and racism. Simultaneously, it is the same totalitarian overcoat worn inside out. 'Why is he your friend? Because he is a stranger!'.

Whether your attitude towards a stranger should be kind or sceptical must however, and this is the gist of the liberal idea, be assessed according to the situation. The matrix proposed by multiculturalists and radical conservatives is useless. Generally, scepticism of the stranger is unwarranted. But only as a rule. Suspicion towards the unknown is not politically suspect. Friends and family have passed a test while strangers are still being tested. Right-wing extremists draw on imagined threats and their narrow-minded and self-righteous world-view is despicable. But threats may be real. Dissuading women from strolling alone in certain areas of Malmö in southern Sweden is neither 'xenophobic' nor lacking in respect. It shows that I respect those who encourage me to advise her against doing it, because I know that their view is real and must be taken into account. The fact that I might not share their views is another story.

Claiming the right to walk anywhere, anytime, dressed no matter how, addressing anybody whenever you feel like – without considering that others, too, have their freedom, is not tolerant or opposed to xenophobia. It signifies egotism, lack of respect of other cultures and racism in reverse. It is anything but 'multicultural'. Rather than human rights, this attitude is about Western and 'white' supremacy. Some are racists in the ordinary sense of the word. The form of racism discussed here, however, is both unconscious and more sophisticated because it transforms the cultural expression of minorities into an object of our fascination, turning a blind eye to the fact that cultural conviction is something real and not a stage show. Chiefly, Prasad and Prasad maintain, the marriage between diversity and neoliberalism referred to as 'diversity management' is meant to offer 'rainbows and dreams of colourful but empty utopias completely disconnected to the dark side of identity politics and group conflicts'.[254] 'The multiculturalist tolerates the Other', Žižek claims, 'only so long as the *real* other is kept out of the picture for the benefit of the Antiseptic Other full of pre-modern ecological wisdom, fascinating rites etc. – once you talk about the *real* Other (and customs such as genital mutilation) tolerance comes to a stand-still.'[255] What 'are we supposed to do with all these different Others', Aje Carlbom asks, 'who are fascists?'[256] Good question. Historically traded customs do matter, Perry Anderson maintains, 'and the animosities between them are not arbitrary, but rooted' in the fact that doctrines may be incompatible.[257]

Through controlled animosity towards others, we recognise their existence – their customs and traditions, their social patterns and religious orientation. A world view in which all forms of xenophobia are charged with moralism as something inherently negative rests on the opposite conclusion. In other words, we (Westerners) must not bother about overseas cultures, traditions, and social rules – in particular those we find challenging. Multiculturalists assume that only Westerners exist, while others are characters in our global comedy. Our anxiety and hostility can end only if we deny the fact that the Other actually exists. We put our arm around someone who might not like it, and our composure is only paralleled by our arrogance. Animosity towards the unknown implies: I see you, and I respect you. Multicultural rhetoric about xenophobia enables the colonialist to receive salvation without the slightest change of his or her mindset. Moreover, she can do it with a good conscience because she is standing on the right side of the barricades.

I am not omnipotent if I sense animosity against others. I am omnipotent if I live my days and years without ever being afraid and when real life is being transformed into *my experience*; into something 'enriching', and something I can 'bring with me'. Human existence is not a souvenir or a photo in an album. 'Xenophobia' is an expression of human rights in its most colonial form. In order to make the world innocent, we tie it hand and foot, lean back in the wicker chair, and throw allegations at those to whom the world is real and occasionally frightening.

While right-wing populists including fascists and right-wing extremists condemn strangers based on prejudices, diversity advocates approach strangers with blind enthusiasm. To instil authority, racists raise their chin and lower their voice. To deny hierarchy, multiculturalists lower their heads and speak in a higher-pitched voice. Unless you sense animosity towards strangers, the former will brand you as a traitor to your country. Unless you embrace strangers, the latter will mark you as a racist. The discussion is kept 'vibrant and thriving' by individuals with 'an immigrant background', as exemplified on a website of a small Swedish university.[258] It does not matter who it is, as long as the skin colour is the right one and the name poses a challenge. Irrespective of what the stranger does, the right-wing extremist will show no mercy. No matter what the stranger is doing, the multiculturalist remains fascinated. When Mulugeta, our chauffeur in Addis Ababa, made a commonplace observation, my friend and expatriate leans forward from the backseat: 'Oh really?' I get a quick glance from Mulugeta in the driver's mirror as he turns the ignition key.

Diversity at the University and multiculturalism in general makes use of the concept of racism in a most sweeping manner. As a result, right-wing populist parties increase. The fact that xenophobia is a most problematic concept goes unnoticed. In an attempt to put the argument right into the definition, the report discusses at great length 'images of us-and-them'. An image is not a social problem but a psychological one. The idea is anti-racist and fashionably self-critical: there is no 'we'. Those who disagree with the multicultural analysis should be offered information and therapy.

Despite their air of anti-racism, stereotypes are not undermined but underpinned by diversity. As any other multicultural reasoning, the report stresses the need for an ethnic perspective. It is assumed that nationalism is expected to be offset by ethnic diversity because nationalism is a bad thing. But this conclusion is dubious for at least two reasons. First, all kinds of nationalism make the multiculturalist shy away. As a result of this political puritanism, the welfare state has gone missing. Regarding the relation between the nation state and the EU, defenders of diversity have come out of the closet as elitists and anti-democrats. Multiculturalists are neoliberals in case the nation state is a racist entity. The credo of nationalism flows seamlessly, we are told, via *Gemeinschaft* into racism and fascism. This particular danger, other would insist, is merely 'potential'.[259]

The cultural nationalism proposed during the early 19th century by the German romantic Johann Herder; Giuseppe Garibaldi's efforts to unite Italy and, in recent times, Jürgen Habermas' defence of the nation state as a framework for modernity and welfare arrangements all exemplify democratic expressions of nationalism.[260] It remains to be proven why national independence and the rule of law are in fact expressions of right-wing extremism.

Second, in any endeavour to oppose sinister nationalism, ethnic diversity is a most odd companion. Why? Because the discourse of diversity is, in itself, saturated with roots of mysticism and anti-individualism, which, admittedly, at times goes well beyond the subject of its critique. During the Balkan war a new concept was born: ethnic cleansing. In comparison to the political legitimacy of the Habermasian nation state, diversity's ethnicity discourse often has a more ominous, self-righteous tone, partly because this form of ethnicity is lacking in empathy and understanding for other groups. Instead, it is all about 'identity' and 'ethnic pride'. Solidarity is lost because it is – precisely – about respect and understanding for those who are situated outside our own ethnic group – which, in turn, requires a less engaged relation to our heritage. I do not feel a deeper ethnic pride and I believe this is good. Multicultural ethnicity has hierarchical implications because 'we' are seen as better than 'they' – deeper, more important, more tormented and more authentic. Historically, the idea of ethnicity was deeply conservative. It was about creating a unity based on myth and unanimity. All together, these tendencies add fuel to a sense of exclusion and creation of self-mythology and subsequently, a sense of being select, of refinement and superiority coupled with a lack of concern for 'the Other' outside one's own ethnic framework, along with a patronising attitude towards *the enemy within* – minorities and dissidents *inside* the ethnic group.

The fact that diversity contributes to social polarisation rather than anything else can also be illustrated by the 'community leader' – i.e. a prominent individual from a particular ethnic group offering guidance and support to other members of this ethnic group. When *Diversity at the University* refers to community leaders and the necessity to 'recognise yourself', it is neither about intellectual affinity nor emotional proximity, but about a visual sense of recognition. To illustrate: I recognise myself in those who look the way I do. This anti-intellectual impulse of association is dominant in pre-modern and ethno-based cultures and among animals. It is the idea that underscores a division between 'us' and 'them'.

Yet again, multiculturalism has a double agenda. While our sense of 'us' is mere delusion, a sense of 'we' among minority groups is the outcome of an agonising historical experience all the same. Regarding minority groups, multicultural descriptions are rich with political romanticism such as roots, religious myths, authenticity, and organicism, implying absolute concord. Despite its superficial rhetoric, diversity discourse does not prevent images of 'us-and-them'. Rather, diversity is an emblematic *idea* of 'us-and-them'. Us: inside our group. Them: outside our group.

Ultimately, multiculturalism does not rest on ideas, but on morals and geography. Regarding 'us,' any allusion towards cultural antagonism does not even pass the threshold of definition. In terms of 'them', it is no longer about psychological 'images' but about righteous territorial struggles, authenticity, and the like. As noted by George Orwell, this is about 'transferred nationalism' – much the same lack of resilience, fanaticism, and group cult as any classic jingoism – only not *here* but *over there.* In both directions, the rhetoric of 'us-and-them' has racist implications; the ethnic group is swept into a mist of humiliating ethno-mysticism, while the domestic population is prohibited the distinction in terms of a modern and transparent bureaucracy, gender equality, free press and the principle of public access to official records.

As was covered by Anders Persson in his comment to the report, the rhetoric of 'us-and-them' might also be critically examined from a practical viewpoint. He suggests that the critical term 'handling routine', according to which immigrant groups, in contrast to jargon, is subject to systematic social *marginalisation.*[261] We wish to protect 'them' from 'us', and so we construct images of 'us-and-them'. One might paraphrase Faust: 'Always wills the good and always works the bad'.

As an influential movement, biologism had its heyday in the early 20th century. Biologism is a pseudo-scientific version of racism, claiming that human beings are motivated by biological qualities such as skin colour and 'phrenology' rather than by environment. The report brings it up. The question is: How are attempts to define race biologically being countered? Either by showing that biological qualities are an insufficient basis for ethnic belonging, by claiming that DNA-structure, genetic material and related biological qualities do not support a race theory. As a result, natural science is being used *against* racism. Alternatively, biological arguments are not taken into account at all. From this point of view, there is no difference between claiming that our race can be proven by our biology, or insisting that it cannot – because, in both cases, biologism is invited into the discussion and accepted as established science.

Choosing between these two alternatives, the report sides with the former: 'No scientific proof', it is claimed, supports 'the idea that human beings biologically belong to different races' (...) We are all, under the surface, equal or equally different, as presented by *Human Genome*, a large survey of our genetic material'.[262] As an argument against biological science, the report cites biological science. The question is whether one should engage in this discussion at all? True, the cited material did not lend support to the view that human beings biologically belong to different races. But what if we did? Then we would have been trapped by natural science: anti-racists in case nature says so, and racists if the dice turned out otherwise. Natural science is part and parcel of modernity, but when multiculturalists for once take on natural science, it comes out as natural mystique.

Yet again, we are faced with the contradictions of multiculturalism. The best way to counter racism, as pointed out by Bernhard Crick, is to defend equality between groups. *Diversity at the University*, in stark contrast, suggests that racism is best kept at bay by doing much the same, but the other way around – idealising strangers instead of indigeneous Swedes. The most efficient way to confront nationalist sentimentalism is by means of scientific historic enquiry adhering to objectivity, criticism of the sources, and so on. According to multiculturalists, this is a half-measure. Instead they portray countries overseas in kitschy colours, i.e. turn to nationalist sentimentalism *elsewhere*. The most convenient method to counteract right-wing extreme objectives stuffed with biologism is to question the scientific basis of biologism. In the eyes of the diversity advocate, this is all too intellectual. Instead, right-wing radical ideas (biologism) are being applied in order to oppose right-wing radicalism. Images of 'us-and-them' from the viewpoint of Norwegian fjords and Bavarian mountains are being replaced by images of 'us-and-them' from the standpoint of the Ethiopian plateau and the deserts of Kuwait. Beneath the surface, the very critique against rightist tendencies as proposed by multiculturalists is as questionable as the ideas under attack.

There are no genetic differences between ethnic groups, which, to the protagonists of diversity, provides evidence for tolerance. There are no genetic differences in DNA-structure between modern and pre-modern human beings that, in the eyes of the right-wing extremist, offer a sociobiological justification for political violence.

'Colour is skin deep' captures the essence of this idea. This is supposed to be an argument against racism, and the gist of the argument is that we are – physiologically speaking – similar. But why insist that skin texture does not comply with 'frontiers of race'? Yet again the very same biologism – genetic and bodily qualities as basis for political action – is simultaneously attacked and invoked.

In the report, the immigrants' situation during the 1990s was described above as strongly marked by racism, xenophobia, discrimination, and marginalisation, and diversity, we were told, emerged as a response against it. Perhaps these right-wing tendencies instead were fuelled by diversity? But in case the situation actually grew worse as a result of diversity, we must ask: What situation, really? In what sense was Sweden of the 1990s strongly marked by racism? I see in front of me marching young men and a society in a state of disintegration. Sweden is not a stainless society. The teenagers John Hron and Gerard Gbeyo were both murdered in 1995, and Björn Söderberg, an active syndicalist, was killed in 1999.

In both cases the murderers were skinheads. Still, the description is nevertheless unfair. Sweden's immigration policy includes policy measures, reports, educational projects, internships, integration efforts, adjustment guides, immigrant quotas and other forms of political measures. In case Sweden was marred by racism, and its state apparatus in tatters, we would probably not engage in projects such as *Diversity at the University*. What is the reason behind this self-criticism? I suggest two reasons, and they both call attention to the relation between diversity and racism.

The first reason behind this self-criticism is linked to George Orwell's notion of 'negative nationalism' – an everyday nationalist self-obsession, characterised by the fact that your country is not blindly admired but effortlessly condemned. Negative nationalism, Orwell maintains, is about liberal post-colonial guilt being expressed through an irrepressible desire to criticise your own country and culture. However, Sweden in the 1990s was not racist but fairly generous towards immigrants and asylum seekers. In case negative nationalism under the surface exhibits a mere mirror image of classic nationalism, 'reverse racism' is identical to classic racism, save for the fact that the object of collective humiliations is no longer 'the Other' but us. They are not the ones who are narrow-minded, selfish, and brutal, who have a superficial and empty culture, but we who are xenophobes, and ours is a culture accessible only via parodies. The allegations have not changed, but the storm is blowing in the other direction.

The second reason why Sweden is described as 'marred by racism' is linked to another branch of Europe's liberal post-colonial guilt, namely the view that – against the background of our history – immigrant groups would be provoked and offended by national pride. We are, hence, fabricating a model of other cultures constituted by our oppression.

Their colour and ambience is supplied, not by them, but by us. We lock them in not only in their culture but also in their past. We equate suffering with spiritual refinement. The greater the suffering, the greater the calls for revenge, and the more futile the prospects for integration, the deeper and more majestic we perceive it. Through their despair and their hatred against us, minority groups offer us a sophistication we do not have.

But this image of immigrant groups is not true. By and large, human beings from overseas are not unable to differentiate between weak and strong nationalism – between the group as protection and the group as war machine. People from weak states are more attached to the group than we are. Immigrants do not oppose Swedish traditions. Much like negative nationalism as a whole, diversity's view of Sweden as racist is primarily our own fictitious construct. At the same time as being proud anti-racists, we sense a slight excitement through collective self-harassment. Foreign cultures are less focused on our historical injustices than we might think. In Vietnam, not many want to talk about the war against the Americans. We may despair at the fact that they wish to move on, but that is the way it is. Amidst the multicultural humbleness I sense a certain machismo. Will overseas cultures remain permanently crippled as a result of the pain inflicted by us? Why do we grab them by the throat? Have we not hurt them enough? A friend in Hanoi who spent many years as 'elite youth' in the Soviet Union deplores the fact that the Americans lost the war. 'South Korea, you know, very much like Vietnam at the time.' She senses my reaction and smiles.

The problem is not when we express modest national pride but when we do not. Emotionally, it is hard to explain. First, why can we not enjoy our culture when all others can? Second, why should immigrants feel offended by national pride? This humbly patronising attitude well illustrates our sense of superiority. On a deeper level, our lack of self-esteem and constant lust for unfavourable comparisons reveal, as a third case in point, a quite majestic self-image, as if we do not need that piece of turf vital for lower races. They call it pasture, we call it xenophobia. We throw dirt on our own country as a sign of our privilege. Ethereal and intangible, smiling indulgently at those whose passport lasts more than a year, we jet-set from one 'genuine experience' to another supplied by attentive locals. 'The politically correct narrow elitist upper-middle-class' of today, Slavoj Žižek comments, does not only oppose 'itself to the majority of common people', but they are in addition 'despised for being caught in their narrow ethnic or community confines'.[263] We dress down and brag about our misery. Fat and in rags we stagger in and out of night clubs in Jakarta while the glass doors are opened by poor boys and girls wearing robes shining in gold and orange.

We are reckless and therefore omnipotent. Fourth, their frustration, paralysis, and hatred towards us makes us exited – a good case of a master-slave relationship. As a result of this paralysis, integration becomes a dead-end, and yet again Anders Persson's 'handling routine' comes to mind. The Swedish ministries fabricate tragedy around the immigrant, giving meaning to our uneventful lives.[264] Fifth, why should immigrants respect and honour Swedish culture when we cannot do so ourselves? Sixth, we seem to believe that tensions between groups are abstract constructs to be averted by means of a theoretical invention. For refugees, however, conflicts are political realities about state, family structure, and freedom of speech. Our trivialisation of political conflicts is naive and ethnocentric. How would political refugees respond if they were asked to work on their images of 'us and them'?

The entire multicultural edifice of xenophobia is not 'anti-racist'. Rather, it is a good example of Western arrogance at its most hypocritical, presumptuous, and intellectually confused. The diversity advocate reaches out his hand, saluting the death of the family and the blessing of the stranger. Whether the greeting is successful or not is anybody's guess.

Diversity at the University makes a historical comment on racism: 'The concept of race', it is maintained, 'emerged during the 19th century'.[265] Diversity has other origins. Racism and diversity share, however, common roots in the Romantic movement and the revolt against the Enlightenment of the early 19th century: where nation, ethnicity, and race were seen as in themselves complete and finalised in the revolt against Human Rights; in language mysticism, ethnic-nationalist self-haughtiness and a world-view characterised by pessimism and sentimentality.[266] These ideas of the immense variation of human mentality over time, and the idea of holism, whereby any one culture could be understood, not by its isolated parts but only as one organic entity – offered a tremendous source of inspiration to Franz Boas, a classic anthropologist and often cited in both camps. His First World War appeal is worth citing: we must 'understand and respect the *individuality* of other nations'[267] (my emphasis). Another common trait is constituted by the attack against the autonomous individual and her rights. Third, they both propose value relativism – whereby morality in pessimistic fashion is limited in time and space; where cultural interaction is marked by language barriers and confusion of tongues; and where – as a classic case of conservative thinking – any judgment seeking to 'trespass' a cultural border becomes invalid.

Analytically and practically, the concept of ethnicity is inseparable from nationalism. The overlaps put a question mark around the entire morality of ethncity. 'Ethnic cleansing' is one of them. Whether it goes under the name of right-wing extremism or diversity, collectivist ideas about 'us-and-them' are fundamental in any form of political idealism. Yet, reports, papers, dissertations, documents, and conferences go by the thousands where ethnicity is being defended and nationalism is subject of critique. I do not question the good intentions of the multiculturalist. But I question the analysis.

In any endeavour to counter racism, the discourse of diversity is ill-suited. Increased tensions and racism on the rise do not occur *despite* multiculturalism, but, largely, as a *direct result* of it. The fact that anti-racism constitutes the showpiece of multiculturalism is one of its great triumphs because the rhetoric of diversity provides you with practically anything you need for a set-up of a racialized society.

Pedestals, populism and pseudo radicalism

Diversity leads to quality, that's what we're told in the report. But this is not supported by evidence. The University is supposed to 'mirror' society's ethnic mixture. But why and what for? Diversity is said to go well together with internationalisation, and is squarely opposed to racism. Neither argument is convincing. A thorough discussion about connections to neoliberalism is, conclusively, missing.

Three loose themes suggesting that more is obscured than revealed by the report will be discussed. First, as a rule, sources and analyses are biased. Second, arguments are often emotional. Third, the presentation is characterised by an irrational version of populism – irreconcilable factors are combined for greater effect.

We are told that during the course of the project a number of 'interviews, conversations, visits and seminars' were conducted. The purpose was to 'show the ethnic diversity in higher education and measures taken in order to increase it'. Revolving around the common ambition to 'increase (…) ethnic diversity', a 'special survey of different EU-projects' was conducted. In addition, the report 'kept assembling information about other projects of relevance', among them diversity projects in the Finance Department and a study of the efforts to increase ethnic diversity by the Swedish National Agency for Higher Education. The report has been inspired by research at International Migration and Ethnic Relations (IMER).[268] Rather than 'to penetrate these areas entirely', the report's authors maintain, 'we have decided to limit our interest to a few Swedish reports of great significance'.[269]

The material is ambitious and yet ideological. The discourse of diversity is being defended by all sources cited. The biased nature of the report suggests hegemonic power combined with intellectual disorientation, where the latter is covered up by the former – standard practise in authoritarian systems. Why was a more scientifically rigorous picture of this intriguing discussion of no interest to Boel Flodgren, Thomas Östros, Göran Persson and Mona Sahlin? Why not bring some of the counter-arguments into the picture – in particular, as the benefits of diversity were so strikingly obvious?

As a matter of fact, some EU-reports disagree with the overwhelming benefits of diversity and multiculturalism. Why are these papers 'irrelevant'? In a EU-report written by the author of this book, the question was: What is the proper method to increase political participation and voting among immigrant groups in Europe? A liberal model was compared with a multicultural model, and, as the empirical material suggested, separate political organisation along the lines of multiculturalism proved *less efficient* as opposed to a liberal model, where immigrants – in the name of citizens – were invited into *already existing* political organisations.[270] In terms of political engagement, specific 'Pakistani labour movements' constituted, for instance, a relative hindrance. The result was social integration within that group, but not necessarily within society. Are reports such as this one irrelevant because they reach other conclusions? Interest was limited to reports of 'great significance'. Based on what criteria? And says who? I lecture about the dangers of hidden sources. Why should I?

At this point, it should be admitted that the report is not all black-and-white. Dissenting voices do exist. We have already touched upon Yehudi O. Webster's *Against the Multicultural Agenda – A critical Thinking Alternative.* Then again, what is the purpose? As will be remembered, Webster advocates knowledge for its own sake instead of the production of ideology; knowledge, in other words, *how* to think instead of *what* to think, and criticism based on science rather than on morality. This, however, is an ample description of what the report does not contain. Webster is therefore used as an alibi and nobody cares about what he is saying: on the surface respect and inclusion, and under it oppression and marginalisation. Exercising power in this conservative fashion, the German Marxist Herbert Marcuse argues, is 'repressive tolerance'. Another case of bias has to do with the question: By what is our educational career chiefly influenced? It was earlier noted that the overwhelmingly most important aspect was class, and that ethnicity, in comparison, was of minor importance. Yet again, however, a crucial aspect vanishes before you know it. As an undercurrent, throughout the report, we are told that immigrants' under-representation in the educational system is caused by 'prejudices', 'discrimination', and 'marginalisation'. Interestingly enough, class as an explanatory factor does not support the general picture. Why, then, is it left out? Because, I assume, the report would have been cancelled. Anders Persson, one of the authors of the report, expressed concern about the fact that they were told to treat class and ethnicity 'as one'. The analytical precision was lost. What is the point of hiring experts, Lennart Lundqvist wonders, 'when you ignore their expertise?'[271] The situation of immigrants, as shown in *Diversity at the University*, is a mere facet in a wider class complex: 'When social background is taken into account, the net negative effect of ethnicity is weak'.[272] And yet it is all about ethnicity? In case ethnicity fails to explain our level of education, why, then, does it explain everything else? Perhaps, instead the situation in the educational sector indicates a general phenomenon, namely how class towers above any other explanatory factor – including ethnicity. The 'Swedish government', as cited in the report, 'has decided to implement a law (...) against ethnic discrimination at work (SFS 1999:130), calling for pre-emptive measures in state authority'. While the explanatory power of ethnicity is close to zero in education, it has legal ramifications in work life.

Immigrants' situation on the job market, right-wing extremists say – as spellbound by ethnicity as are multiculturalists – is not much different than for anybody else. This is not true. These individuals, as correctly pointed out in the report, often have 'significant barriers to overcome' before they can finally adjust in Sweden.[273] Still, in case your class situation is the key factor, immigrants' problems are linked to lower education and working class background. Immigrants' situation on the job market is of course something to be concerned about, but those with poor education will always struggle on the job market. Swedish working class individuals are advised to get an education, and cannot play the card of marginalisation.

Foreigners in the labour force are, on the contrary, recommended to blame their misfortunes on others, creating additional problems for minority groups. Oppositional groups are sliced into handy bits by the pseudo-radical knife of diversity; not much is left of the common working class struggle. The Swedish Law of Employment Protection - resting on 'Last in, first to go' - is left out in the report. Why is not ethnicity as an explanation for exclusion compared to legalised employment protection, dissuading employers to hire new staff no matter from where they come? Perhaps because this legislation further questions the influence of ethnicity – dearly embraced by multiculturalists and right-wing extremists alike?

Above, the focus was on the report's scientific bias. Next, we shall deal with rhetoric based on emotions, such as moralism and related irrational criticism.

One of the pillars of *Diversity at the University* is the idea that 'shared understanding goes up and ethnic prejudices goes down (...) as a result of an increased mixture of cultures in higher education'.[274] The statement is passionate, and nothing but. The relation between 'presence' and tensions is most intricate. Some say that shared territory is good, other say it is bad. In the eyes of a Serb or a Croat, the idea that co-existence is all it takes is nothing but a dark joke. Claiming, on the other hand, that co-existence will inevitably lead to conflict overlooks the fact that a 'mixture of cultures' often, indeed, is quite unproblematic. This is the opposite cliché constantly repeated by right-wing extremists. One being pitch-dark and the other one exceedingly optimistic, both conclusions emanate from the totalitarian drafting table.

Instead of being caused by 'prejudices', the reason behind critiques against other ethnic groups may simply be the fact that reality is challenging, perhaps getting out of hand. A serene and harmonious co-existence will soon come about, we have a habit of saying, if we only overcome our 'prejudices'. But this is nothing short of psychological blackmail, and can only be obtained if we erase our memory and history completely – if human beings are *made anew*. Left-wing disorientation has reached new heights when critiques in between ethnic groups are deemed as right-wing extremism. At this point, in the middle of all postmodernist and relativist jargon, multiculturalists advocate for a rigorous universalism, where groups under siege who seek to retain *their truth* are shown little if any understanding.

Those chiefly hit by diversity's rhetoric about ethnic prejudices are, precisely, conservative minority groups in which – unlike in the West – relativism, decadence, modernity, and self-criticism have limited influence. Critique against the Enlightenment is a product *of* the Enlightenment endured by few. For those who have not yet experienced modernity – whose world-view is concrete, antagonistic, limited to one physical territory, and above all deeply emotional – the very idea of a 'prejudice' is an attack against existence as such. While the idea of 'prejudice' might appear relativistic and 'anti-West', it threatens to undermine precisely those traditional life-forms unprotected against Western relativism and modernity. Behind the paper-thin humility, the concept of ethnic 'prejudice' demonstrates the West's contempt for cultures where the homestead does not mean fascism, but your place on Earth.

The report has a lot to say about 'others' prejudices. But what about its own conclusions? Are they always well substantiated? 'Quite simply', we are told that under 'Diversity in education and teaching', 'a greater ethnic diversity among students should be accompanied by a greater diversity in education and teaching'.[275] 'Ethnic diversity among researchers brings in more perspectives and experiences. The connection between diversity and quality is therefore self-evident'.[276] 'In terms of *the social quality dimension*', the report initially maintains, 'increased social quality is likely to follow upon more diversity because (…) ethnic diversity is a good thing'.[277] As a concept, 'diversity as a resource' is 'about being conscious about diversity as a resource in higher education, and our efforts to make use of it in this fashion'.[278] Various national efforts to boost diversity are the focus under 'International outlook', and 'Great Britain, the Netherlands, Germany, and Sweden are portrayed as role models."[279]

It is all about common sense: conclusions are 'self-evident', and arguments are 'quite simply' obvious. This line of reasoning, however, characterised the ruling right during the 19th century. The fact that this approach has been taken over by the multiculturalists says a lot about the power shift of late. What is 'self-evident' about 'greater diversity' resulting from 'increased ethnic diversity among students?' Why must a blue-eyed Swede be taught by a blue-eyed teacher? Irrespective of their origin, working class students, as repeated in the report, are confronted by similar obstacles. Any talk about ethnic homogeneity is, moreover, challenged by the fact that some individuals are surgeons or art-collectors, while others are fishermen and illiterate.

Researchers with another skin colour, we are told, increase quality. Why is this 'self-evident'? Why cannot 'increased quality' (however defined) be supplied by a Swedish researcher? What is wrong with us? Why not instead try to find out what we write and think? The university is not a racial institute. Regarding *the social quality dimension*, Google only has five hits, three among them from *Diversity at the University*. Why use italics as if you cite an academic tradition when you are only referring to yourself? The reason why quality is increased by diversity is, it is maintained, because ethnic diversity is 'a good thing'. This looks like circular evidence to me.

Naturally, diversity can be 'a good thing'. But this has nothing to do with whether you are aware or not. Those to whom diversity is a political atavism are as conscious as anybody else. They have only reached different conclusions. In the report's international outlook, certain countries – among them Sweden – 'are seen as role models'. By whom?

The report tries to undermine dissenting views by playing the prejudice card, and yet emotional rhetoric fills the pages. This must not, however, be deemed as prejudices, because the diversity advocate argues on behalf of oppressed minorities. Multiculturalists are therefore licenced to say just about anything, and the more pompous and unfounded the better, because this merely shows the acuteness of the situation of minorities, which in turn shows how right they are. A lot has happened since the intellectualism of the old left and its struggle on behalf of the oppressed majority.

As a rule, reports of ambition contain a substantial discussion about their central premise. *Diversity at the University* is chiefly about ethnic diversity, but is ethnicity subject to any clarifying analysis? Not as far as I can see. A short note under 'Diversity' is as close as its gets: 'The question why emphasis is on class at some point, gender at another, and ethnicity at yet another point in time is one of life's interesting riddles'. The report continues, 'there are intricate reasons of global as well as national character as to why ethnicity of late has gained such a strong influence but this,' the sentence suddenly ends, 'is nothing we shall discuss any further'.[280] *Diversity at the University* was not just any document. In its scope and impact as a governmental report advocating diversity, it is probably unique. The unparalleled influence of diversity in higher education was, moreover, a direct result of the universities' diversity plans – in turn a direct outcome of the Social Democratic government report entitled *Diversity at the University.* Today this bold and radical ideology has merged with the state. But the reason behind it is of no interest.

As a final case of scientific flaws, we will touch upon various populist tendencies in the report. As a classic example, the late Jörg Haider, former party leader of the Austrian Freedom Party, had the habit of addressing the blatantly unfair (i.e. not high enough) wages for anyone from farm hands to EU-bureaucrats. Advocating increased wages for everybody is, in case politics is about redistribution, no longer strictly about politics.[281] The report's similar populist tendencies are, on the one hand, about connecting diversity to a wider national community – the welfare state – and, on the other hand, linking it up with the individual, society's smallest entity.

Diversity at the University contains many positive references to the welfare state. Compulsory school attendance of 1842 enabled 'capitalism and eventually a welfare state society'.[282] 'In the distribution of welfare', inequalities are levelled out and democracy is protected by education.[283] Education and research are important in order to 'develop the Swedish welfare state'.[284] 'The social segregation of immigrants has been stabilised on a high level', as cited in *Committee for The Year End Report on Welfare closure* (*Kommittén Välfärdsbok-*

slut).[285] 'The greatest common task for our country right now', the report maintains, is to profit from this diversity, 'where people with various ethnic background live and work together on equal terms, respecting each other's specific nature'.[286]

In the report, the welfare state is properly defended. Still, an analysis cannot carry just about everything. If so, science drifts towards populism. The premises of ethnicity, diversity, and multiculturalism contradict the ideas of the welfare state. The welfare state is linked to the idea of the rule of law and *equal rights before the law*. This idea is being undermined by the rhetoric of diversity and 'the rights of the enclave', where minority groups may follow laws based on custom and culture. The welfare state has a political foundation based on equal rights *irrespective* of culture, religious, class-based, or any other belonging. Diversity has a cultural basis, and walls tower between 'us' and 'them'. The secular nature of the welfare state enables religious pluralism and 'diversity'. The cultural nature of ethnicity makes the separation between the spiritual and worldly power more difficult, and as a result religious pluralism is stifled.

The welfare state is constructed around solidarity, and the key political instrument is constituted by the notion of class. Multiculturalists speak silently about class, but all the more about ethnicity. While the welfare state is egalitarian and rationalist, diversity is hierarchical with an aura of myth. As any culturally-based theory, diversity is a rightist idea and the welfare state is moderately left-wing; while the welfare state originally emanates from reformist socialism and liberalism, ethnicity, under the progressive surface, is conservative with its roots in early 19th century romantic counter-Enlightenment. The dark shadow of nationalism is looming large over the rhetoric of diversity. The election of political representatives in a modern welfare state is based on formal qualifications. As a consequence of this, self-idealisation is reduced and citizens' influence is fostered. In ethnic minority groups, representatives are often appointed by means of romantic-mythical reasons such as 'shared historical experience'. Political transparency is undermined. The representative is hence transformed into *la volonté générale* –

the voice of the silent herd and a famous image of the authoritarian system. Grounds for decision-making banned in the welfare state are common within ethnic minority groups. The welfare state rests on the progressive idea of *equality*. The multicultural idea – as shown by the prefix 'multi' – is based on the notion of *inequality*, and the more unequal, odd, out-of-the-ordinary, dissenting, exotic, and bizarre, the better; which, in turn, rests on the expectation that increased cultural distance fuels tolerance, respect, and 'curiosity', only to reach its climax when a sense of alienation is complete. At that point a kind of engagement emerges: intellectual and controlled, and yet reckless and emotional. Cultural diversity spills over into economic diversity which explains why the idea of diversity has gained such a wide footing among neoliberals.

A document entitled *Welfare Closure* is cited even though the analytical premises of the welfare state are incompatible with diversity. The welfare state rests, as rightly pointed out in the report, 'on the idea of equality'. But why confuse this with diversity? Diversity is about the benefits associated with being different. The more diversity, the less room for welfare state solutions. The more myth, the less modernity. A Marxist does not support the monarchy, and a liberal does not wish the bank to be owned by the state. But multiculturalists may seemingly drag anything they wish into their populist, all-embracing scheme without anyone taking notice.

More often, however, diversity is associated, not with an outer political framework, but with the individual. It should be stated clearly that the report does contain various clarifying discussion on this topic. The power of the group clashes with the autonomy of the individual. As a result of a 'collective struggle for recognition', 'group identities' may come about where no other 'particular nature is allowed than the one sanctioned by the group'.[287] The report cites K. A. Appiah's analysis, where the individual traits of group members might go missing as a result of a persistent focus on the 'recognition' of collective group rights. In case, as firmly demanded by the multicultural politics of recognition, 'skin colour and sexuality is expected to take on a political role, it gets increasingly hard for those who wish to treat their skin and sexual body as nothing but personal dimensions of the self'.[288]

As a rule, however, this principled conflict is obscured by optimism. Today, when diversity is on the agenda, we are told, 'it is about diversity in society, which mainly is linked to the fact that a human being can manifest itself in a great variety of ways'. This variety 'may be traced back to various factors we chose to focus on – biological, economic, cultural, political and so on – when differences between human beings are being registered, socially constructed and defined.'[289] An earlier governmental report within the field of integration is brought to attention under a heading entitled 'Critically and independently thinking individuals': 'As has been pointed out, individual and group identity are of great significance in multicultural society, and in the government bill on integration the inherent worth of a strong individual identity in a multicultural society was being emphasised.' 'The importance of an open and vibrant discussion, and of tolerance along with creativity and fearlessness' was emphasised.[290]

In different ways, the report emphasises individual choice as a basis for various group identities: 'A construction of identity resting on the fact that individuals unite through group identities based on individual choice occur wherever human beings differ'.[291] 'Ever since the 1980s', the reports maintains, 'the multicultural criticism has turned strongly individualistic whereby cultural belonging is seen chiefly at the discretion of the autonomous individual'.[292] Diversity and free choice of the individual are fused after a historical comment: 'Since the 1950s, Sweden has developed into a multicultural society. The guiding principle of our new cultural integration policy emanating during the 1990s, is the preservation of cultural identity and the individual's right to freely select cultural belonging.'[293] As above: diversity depends on what people 'choose to emphasise'.

In the presentation, there is no tension between diversity and individuality. The pages are filled with 'the choice of the individual, and the guiding principle' is diversity in alliance with the autonomous individual. But is it really so? The picture is not quite accurate, even if we make a comparison with voluntary associations. In a chess club, for instance, you cannot oversleep on a Sunday morning when your team is playing. There is a price to pay even in an apolitical association. This is the point of group membership: You *surrender* your independence for the benefit of something else.

The trouble with ethnic belonging is not the fact that individuals wander astray in a forest of cultural and religious opportunities. Real life – i.e. outside the ivory towers of academia – is not about postmodern ethno-shopping. In practise, diversity is not 'a social construct' or 'creative', but a poetically appealing battle-cry on behalf of the ethnic group – a sentimental reaction fused with romanticism and myth. If you can combine postmodernity and diversity, you can combine anything. According to the entire critique against diversity, individual choice *is stifled* by the rhetoric of ethnicity.

> "Culture", argue Eriksen and Stjernfelt, "is a package, take it or leave it, you can't pick and choose as you please. Clearly, individuals freedom to assemble their own menu of cultural aspects is circumscribed, but communication between cultures also comes to a standstill because all character traits of the individual are said to be provided by our unique culture."[294]

Did the report fail to notice this discussion? Is it perhaps *not relevant* because it reaches other conclusions? Mixing diversity and 'critical and independent individuals' is cynical. Multiculturalism, argues the German-Turkish author Seyran Ates in *The Multicultural mistake – What to do in order to live better together in Germany* (*Der Multikulti-Irrtum – Wie wir in Deutschland besser zusammenleben können*) is a mistake precisely because the German state makes it a virtue to separate people from each other.[295] Ates was severely beaten and forced to close her Berlin law office where she had been working with young Muslim women who had been subject to violence. Early 2013 she once again opened her office, but she has a security guard during public appearances. Did, then, all of this happen because Ates lost a sense of direction in her all-to-diversified independence? Why did the American journalist and author Christopher Hitchens oppose religion? What was the fatwa against Salman Rushdie really about? I could keep counting. As noted by Per

Bauhn and Dilsa Demirbag-Sten, multiculturalists do not shy away from suddenly ignoring 'the ethnic culture' for the sake of avoiding critique: 'Either, an aggregate level is deployed in order to sidestep questions about honour crime'. 'This is about what men in general are doing to women in general.' Or, the perspective is from the standpoint of the individual: 'This is merely an issue of mentally disturbed men.' In both cases, you stay clear of a discussion about the level of culture situated in between – normally a perspective never abandoned by the multiculturalist.[296] The switch of ethnicity is turned on regarding dance and food, and turned off when unpleasant things are on the table. In the name of honour, Fadime Sahindal was shot in the head by her father in Uppsala, Sweden, in 2002. Tell Fadime in heaven 'it is the right of the individual to chose cultural belonging'. Multicultural life, we are told, is characterised by 'fearlessness'. Well, we have freedom of speech. Rumy Hasan sees it differently, and his view warrants quoting in full:

> A woman who breaks free from a forced marriage can expect to be hunted down by 'bounty hunters', private detectives, or organised gangs of networks of men, be intimidated by them and forced to return home, where she will inevitably face further punishment. And she may end up paying the ultimate price for her disobedience: death. This was the tragic fate of Tasleem Begum from Bradford who, after leaving her husband from a forced marriage, was shot in the head by her brother-in-law (who, no doubt in the name of multiculturalism, had his sentence commuted from murder to manslaughter on the grounds of 'provocation' – presumably stemming from the 'shame' and 'dishonour' she had brought his family). Scandalously, religious leaders, though not condoning this, asserted that 'according to the Koran, killing this woman was correct'. (…) Suffice to say that the signal this gives out to women contemplating deviating from the path chosen for them is enormously powerful. Moreover, it is a clear illustration of the often prohibitively high 'exit costs' (reaching life-threatening proportions) from a religious ethnic community.[297]

The benefits of ethnic belonging are cooperation and unity. The disadvantages are lack of freedom and oppression; the loss of individuality.[298] The advantage of liberalism and individualism is the free choice of the individual and her independence. The downsides are a sense of loneliness and social anomie. With unflinching energy, multiculturalism defends the group as one and undivided. It is therefore not only collectivist, but also closely linked to Marxism and conservatism. The individual is reduced to a cog and part of the whole, be it machine or organism, nation, race or class. As a theory, then, diversity is incompatible with liberalism, where the single individual constitutes the core of analysis, and where utopia and collectivist ideas are treated with the utmost scepticism. Multiculturalism is brimming with utopianism and idealism such as the internal harmony of the ethnic group, and the idea that tensions between groups can be overcome by means of administration and information.

Originally, diversity emerged as a theoretical critique against 'the illusion' of 'individual choice', and the liberal and pluralist idea of 'one person – one vote'. In reaction to an 'oppressive majority', minorities started claiming identities and choices based on group. There is much positive to be said about this collectivist struggle, not the least the emergence of a black middle-class in America.[299] Possibly, Martin Luther King saved America from ending up as South Africa. Still, what happens to collectivist mobilisation if minority theory is infused with strong individualism? You eat the cookie or you do not. Why so reckless? Probably out of a feeling of omnipotence, and a concomitant populist conviction that diversity is simply a bucket to be filled with just about anything 'of importance' that may 'broaden our understanding' of its virtues. The relation between the three of these is still antagonistic, even if the report trivialises 'the field of tension of identity politics between individual, group, and society.'

Previously, diversity sought to embrace everything from individual to welfare state. Another case of populism has to do with idealisation and helplessness, i.e. simultaneously wrapping contradictory clichés around an ethnic community. 'In public perception of immigrants, we feel', the report maintains, 'that a certain clientilism has come about, in which they are seen as people in need of help'. It is, therefore, 'of utmost importance for the future of Sweden' to see immigrants 'as an indisputable resource, to the work force and society at large'.[300] Our future 'rests in the hands of' the immigrant. The report is part of a strongly idealising tradition within multiculturalism. Ethnic minorities are honoured as a 'positive potential' in state bureaucracies, in organisations and in political parties. Immigration is 'enriching', and immigrants are 'fascinating'. Diversity brings 'added value', and 'opens doors'. The ethnic minority, the report says, is 'a resource'. 'Xenophilia – We love immigrants!' is announced on a house gable by a communal project in the city of Malmö. A company called *Xenofilia* is soon to move its headquarters to Rosengård in Malmö. The headline says: 'Sweden will be spiced-up by Rosengård.'[301]

Simultaneously, however, the situation of the immigrant is acute. The immigrants cannot make it on their own but are in need of support, comfort, confirmation, and empathy. They are extremely fragile, and hence jokes *of any kind* are out of the question. Those arriving in Sweden will be subject to structural racism, xenophobia, islamophobia, and we advise them to take shelter behind their community leader. Protected by ethnic fortification, they will soon be versed in historical cases of injustice and end up safely alienated from Swedish society. They end up precisely as 'helpless clients' and the multicultural entourage rushes to their defence. Multiculturalism and *Diversity at the University* bear a heavy mark of this stifling empathy.

The multicultural attitude towards immigrants oscillates between crippling compassion and pathetic idealisation. In both cases the ethnic group is assigned qualities it does not have and also cannot have. The ethnic community is, in both cases, caught in a stereotype both glaring and unforgiving. This is all nothing but the projections of the diversity protagonists – revealing that they do not know what they talk about and do not want to know. Like Friedrich Engels a hundred years before, George Orwell wanted to gain insight into the British proletariat, and spent, therefore, some time in a mid-England mining district. The citation above is worth reiterating: Orwell knew enough of the working class not to idealise it.[302] Non-European immigrants are, in contrast, beyond the pale, allowing for humiliating kitsch in any direction.

Belgians are a group of individuals, and therefore, clearly, you cannot say that Belgians are 'fascinating'. But the ethnic group is beyond reach. Opinions about animals are opinions about the group and not about a particular animal, as in I prefer dogs to cats. The multicultural image of the immigrant is, in a similar fashion, not based on specific individuals, but on 'the immigrant' as a species or, if you like, a race. These racist implications loom under a thin veil of multicultural so-called anti-racism.

For the sake of empathy or admiration, the immigrant is put on a pedestal. We: down here. They: up there. Diversity flickers between blind enthusiasm and suffocating pity, and you witness, it seems, a postcolonial upper class soothing its conscience and ignorance with humanistic jargon. The immigrant is *different*, original or awkward, clumsy or fascinating, virile or ethereal, victim or Jack-of-all-trades. Gently, they are removed from our community, furnished with labels, and made into our delight and objects of our opinions and discriminations. We make sure they are not lost in the crowd because this would be tantamount to oppression and majority violence, and to render them invisible. Instead we *acknowledge* them, and they feel *acknowledged*, and when we approach 'the Other', you are witnessing 'a conversation across cultural borders' sterile as salicylic cotton. 'Our task', Malmö University's diversity plans maintains, 'is to create a good work environment where everyone is acknowledged'.[303] We single them out, make them special, unique, one of a kind – in other words subject them to exclusion. When 'the Other' is seen as 'an object and as something completely without self-determination' an 'imperialist attitude can be maintained'.[304] In this practise of selection and division, diversity resembles racism.

In both cases, we are witnessing Westerners sinking their soul into one or another caricature. The multiculturalist and the racist are as keen to separate 'us' from 'them'. Racism can only come about by making the stranger different from us. Diversity can only come about if the immigrant is portrayed as different from us – as a 'resource' or as an innocent victim of our racism. More still: racism is the emotional climax on a situation where the stranger has been deprived of his resemblances with us; i.e. of his human nature. We are human beings; those who lack resemblance to us are not human. Racism does not rule out fascination. Racism is fascination of *a certain kind.* To be held in contempt, something must first be acknowledged. Racism is fascination taken to its logical conclusion. The multiculturalists fail to notice the inherent worth of disinterestedness, to blend in and vanish in the crowd. The multiculturalist has abandoned Martin Luther King's 'colour-blind society'.[305] It does not matter whether the ethnic group is portrayed as victims or as heroes, as long as a postmodern image of 'us-and-them' is upheld, where they are subject of exclusion and exoticism – put on the pedestal to be honoured, scorned, or drenched with pity.

What, finally, is the nature of that suffocating unit against which the ethnic breakaway takes place? Who desires to leave and why? At first sight, the report is concerned about the norm as a principle, and sides with the norm breakers. In a variety of ways, the power of the minority and the right to form dissenting factions are defended, while enforced normality is criticised. 'Processes of standardisation threatening various specific types',[306] 'enforced integration',[307] and 'societal models of integration forcing individuals to abandon or hide various aspects of their identity' are all cause for great concern.[308] Differences are 'to be extinguished for the benefit of unity in (what is referred to as) society'.[309] 'Distinguishing features in particular cultures must not, we are told, 'be erased'.[310] In Roth's *The limits of Diversity* (*Mångfaldens gränser*), a more optimistic picture is cited: 'Today we are witnessing an increased self-confidence among groups who earlier felt they were being silenced and discriminated against'. They might eventually succeed, but persistent efforts are required: 'Group members demand their identities to be acknowledged and affirmed.' They aspire for a situation where human beings' 'particular traits are being respected and affirmed'. The objective of the strategy is 'to counteract ambitions towards assimilation whereby our differences as human beings are ignored or repressed by various majorities'.[311]

It seems that the defence of the minority and the critique against a potentially oppressive majority culture is a *matter of principle*. But this is not quite so. Critical comments about 'standardisation' always target the West. Jeopardised minority groups always cherish 'non-Western' values. The subject of criticism in the entire bag of concepts – ranging from unity, coercion, respect, views being neglected and oppressed, identities abandoned or hidden, over to the historically charged 'annihilation' is of an exclusively Western origin. Why not direct the same principled criticism against those ethnic groups so warmly embraced by the multiculturalists? In case this majestic minority rhetoric is more than words on paper, it must include minorities *of any kind*. Otherwise, one does not really defend minorities as such, but only certain groups into which one has sunk one's personality as against groups of which one does not approve. This is not about ideas or principles or anything remotely related to groups but only about 'I am right and you are wrong and be quiet'. 'Dissenting minorities within ethnic groups', one could write, 'are forced to comply with the views of the majority'. 'Silenced and oppressed women who wish to choose their own partner need to have their rights acknowledged and affirmed'. 'Free-thinking secularists are being oppressed by the ethnic community'. Why not side with the individual per se for once? 'Distinct features characterising the Enlightenment philosophy of certain individual immigrants must not be erased'. Suddenly, however, all breaks are pulled. The multicultural entourage makes a swift U-turn and starts agitating against its previous principles without any sense of inner contradiction. The ethnic community is 'delicate' and marred by 'historical injustice'. Their culture is 'deep', 'holistic', 'organic', 'authentic', and 'will not survive' internal conflicts; a text-book case of political romanticism with a distinct flavour of the 1930s.

The fact that the West is an odd target for this agitated rhetoric about enforced assimilation and differences being annihilated for the benefit of deadening uniformity does not make this case of select rebellion less puzzling. One should be careful not to paint Swedish bureaucracy in rosy colours. Our 'handling routine' in relation to immigrants – as described by Anders Persson above – is a good case of counterproductive measures.[312] But, overall, our attitude towards minorities is still relatively tolerant. By and large, minorities enjoy good protection in Sweden. Regarding this particular critique against patronising majorities, the multiculturalist's own ethnic group is, however, a better case in point. In Sweden, homosexuality has long been accepted, and disrespectful comments will not go unnoticed. This is not the case in all minority groups. The death penalty for blasphemy vanished from Sweden many hundreds of years ago, and yet it is practised in certain religious minorities.

There are many reasons behind this populist blend of group cult and Houdini-like desire to break away. The left-wing upper-middle class was always characterised by a certain exoticism. Foreign cultures are justified because we know next to nothing about them. In contrast, we know a great deal about ourselves, and as a result we are bored stiff. Another reason has to do with the definition of the term 'identity'. Not long ago it was tied to the individual. 'My identity' was about myself and my right and my freedom, and the more identity, the more guts and the more likely to express dissenting views. Today, identity has taken on a different meaning. When you express your identity, says the report and the multicultural *nouvelle gauche*, you must not challenge the general opinion (of your ethnic group). Instead, you must look away, act with 'modesty', and put your will in the hands of the ethnic community leader. 'Freedom', argued the Spartakist and revolutionary Rosa Luxemburg, 'is always exclusively the freedom for those who think differently'. The classic leftist battle for freedom and multicultural neo-conservatives are separated by an abyss.

According to the report, 'processes of modernisation, and standardisation' jeopardise ethnic 'particularities'. This comment is not entirely accidental. As an idea, modern society is about standardisation – i.e. seeking to overcome internal tensions in between groups, create norms, principles and rules – all in order to acquire a functioning state, a legal system, independent institutions, and so on. In the past, Social Democracy used to talk about solidarity irrespective of class, culture, religion, gender, and ethnicity. Behind the progressive mask, the agenda of diversity is from the world of yesterday. The modern idea of society linked to citizenship should be abandoned for the benefit of a pre-modern idea of ethnic belonging and collectivism. When citizenship, multiculturalists claim, is to be replaced by a whirlwind of minority legislation, they seem, Brian Barry comments, 'remarkably insouciant about the abuses and inequities of the *ancien régime* which provoked the attacks on it by the Encyclopaedists and their allies'.[313] When multiculturalists call for a breakaway, it is always a breakaway from modernity. Eriksen and Stjernfelt write: 'In this anthropological prioritisation, modern society along with its culture, civil rights and equality between men and women, falls short of a dusty and romantic ambition in which living prehistory must be preserved in a global *Heimat*-museum. Everything from all times must be allowed to exist in its uncontaminated form simultaneously anywhere.'[314] Through a sense of alienation, we experience mutual understanding.

It is worth adding that when defending modernity, I side with that derided, slow, and grey bureaucrat, because the bureaucrat is, under the lustreless surface, the product of meritocracy and transparency instead of sleazy intimacy. The multicultural criticism against modernity is no less strong here. In Norway, the concept of the day is 'colourful society'. In Sweden, we say 'rainbow society', or 'offices of mosaic'.[315] We show mutual appreciation the way they do on a fashion show. This is an aged form of societal variation, criticised by Max Weber among others, where professional merits are overtaken by eye-catching, animalistic and visual variation. I have already mentioned the ethnic representative who, by virtue of his own physical traits – skin colour and 'phrenological' features among them – is able to dismiss concerns about political qualifications. At this point, it is only a short step to populism, because the populist politicians in the same fashion may dwell in false intimacy, while dismissing demands about formal qualifications for the benefit of something as ominous, as pathetically sentimental as 'shared experience', and jargon like 'I say what you think'. I speak for all of you out there who no longer have a voice, says the right-wing populist with crocodile tears. I speak for all of you out there who have suffered enough, shouts the ethnic representative with his fingers on the wallet. While variation in modernity is abstract and sophisticated, multicultural variety is physical and animalistic. In case multicultural ideology bears all the contours of a reactionary ideology, why not say so? Perhaps, then, a political irony would come to the forefront, namely that the backers of diversity really ought to oppose it, while its assailers – such as *Sverigedemokraterna* – would embrace it if only they gave it a second thought.

A brief critical conclusion of *Diversity at the University* will now follow. Seven themes will be summarised under one common ideology on the political scale of left and right.

First, the definition of diversity is unclear. The rhetoric of diversity appears very different from its qualities and social consequences. Those who fail to understand the virtues of diversity are yet to be informed. This is a totalitarian approach to knowledge. The report tries to replace cultural and other tensions with harmony. Conflict and debate – the university's *raison d'etre*, is openly opposed. Consensus is not an intellectual affair but to be administered therapeutically. In the report, dissenting views are subject to glossy appreciation only to be dismissed at a deeper level. As in any multicultural document, the individual is missing. Multiculturalism, we are told, implies individual free choice. In reality, it is rooted in rigorous collectivism, ethnic mobilisation and the submission of the individual. Through diversity, they say, the university can win acceptance in the eyes of the public. The university is not, then, included in the principle of diversity. Instead, it is subject to ideological ambitions. Recurring, and with great diligence, the report's 'mission' is brought up. *Diversity at the University is*, then, withdrawn from scientific testing. Instead, it is being politicised. The government, as recommended in the report, should feel free to hand out financial support to universities 'in accordance with their success in diversity work.' This uninhibited brutality at least has the virtue of being honest. You want money? Then do as we say. The impression of this paragraph is heavily authoritarian.

Second, ethnic minority groups enrich Sweden, the report keeps reiterating. In so doing, the multiculturalists surprisingly wander deeply into the woods of essentialism. As a rule, multiculturalists scorn essentialists, but then again, we know by now that multiculturalists are not troubled by principles. The picture of ethnic minorities oscillates between helplessness and idealisation. One day they are victims of 'structural racism' and subject to full-scale support, the next day they are 'fascinating and 'enriching'. Either way it is an abstract idea revealing little more than our ignorance. While the right-wing cliché goes: Trust your friends, distrust all others. The left-wing cliché states the opposite. Only in a mind hypnotised by racist categories does the stranger never constitute a threat. What 'we' do not like does not exist. All the agony and the despair characterising overseas cultures is trivialized and bleached into oblivion. All that remains is the jolly stranger bereft of struggle, suffering, longing, content. This attitude is imperialist and exotic.

When ethnic minorities enrich a university, it is also, by implication, not enriched by domestic researchers. By nature, we are 'non-enriching'. The description of Sweden is of a country 'strongly marked by racism'. The report refers to an 'ethnic hierarchy' despite the fact that the situation for ethnic minorities in Sweden is not bad, as a result of our ambitious and fairly successful immigration policy. In this respect, the picture of Sweden is unnecessarily harsh. Some would call it 'reverse racism' – i.e. uncalled for attacks against one's own culture. The paragraph shows a two-fold racist tendency; partly an excessively negative view of the Swedish native population, partly an equally unrealistic, idealised image of ethnic minorities.

Third, *Diversity at the University* displays a one-sided focus on the surface – on optical features, on visual and outer variation, on colour of the skin, and bodily features in general. Rather than human intellectual variation, this is all about character traits that *do not* distinguish us from animals. The modern project – i.e. 'to liberate human beings from being defined by our bodies' – is crumbling before our eyes.[316] Proximity and animosity is instead the task of the 'community leader' and 'ethnic representative'. Identification does not come about via values and opinions – political ones among them – but visually through form, skin, hair, ethnicity. I look the way you do: You can rely on me. In its appetite for the eye-catching and sensationalist – such as a cool tie or a colourful dress in combination with a derisive view of the silent crowd and the bureaucrat with her stamp pad – diversity merges with right-wing populism. The tendency is animalistic and 'primitivist' and expresses a longing for the deep and the pristine and also for the superficial and the inhumane.

As number four, ethnicity is being mythologized. Lecturers and students with 'shared roots' are expected to sense a deep affiliation. The fact that class seems to explains everything and ethnicity next to nothing fails to make an impression. Instead, researchers are told to forget what they already know, and ethnicity may, as a consequence, profit from the concept of class. A cultural community reverberating with nationalism may make a show of borrowed plumes from the parlour of the left. The multicultural new leftists oppose the material and economic base in classic leftist class analysis with all their might, and they seek to replace it with its metaphysical superstructure – roots, history, culture, religion, and so on. A horizontal, transgressing and egalitarian solidarity is being substituted by a vertical and hierarchical loyalty resembling nationalism. How come representatives of ethnic minorities may call for shared roots as a basis for their *political* activity when a Westerner with similar ideas would be branded as a right-wing extremist?

As number five, multicultural critiques against processes of modernisation and standardisation sail under false colours. While it may be portrayed as progressive and 'post'-modern, it actually paves the way for the whims and arbitrariness of 19th century class society. Ylva Hasselberg refers to this as a case of 'refeodalisation'.[317] The report speaks warmly about ethnic and cultural differences, but tends to overlook the fact that difference as social principle rests on a long and dark tradition. It did not fade away until the progressive forces at the time – chiefly Social Democrats – managed to push through the principle of equality; between classes, between men and women and so on. *Diversity at the University* tries to link up with internationalisation, although diversity implies a reactive, sentimental hunkering down behind ethnic enclaves, while internationalism is progressive, global and aggressive. In the report, diversity constitutes a radical response to racism. In reality, however, they both emanate from the romantic movement of the early 19th century: in the relativistic idea of impenetrable ethnic enclaves; in the aversion against the individual; in confusion of tongues and self-mythologisation. Diversity does not oppose constructions of 'us-and-them'. Diversity is an idea of 'us-and-them. In this lack of interest for the achievements of modernity, diversity resembles neo-liberalism, another pseudo-radical idea evoking 19th century class society. Additional similarities between the two include a fixation with the surface, intellectual recklessness, aversion against open discussion, and occupations bridging the two fields, such as 'diversity managers'. In one word, this paragraph illustrates pseudo-radicalism. Diversity is old wine in new bottles.

As case number six we are told, 'diversity leads to quality' even though there are no comparisons in support of this view. An organisational culture in which everything is evaluated does not evaluate diversity. The report says nothing about why diversity is important, and yet it is repeated nearly 500 times in 125 pages. Instead, we are told that the benefits of diversity are 'plain to see'. The report combines diversity with the welfare state and the individual but this is not possible. Ruling norms are criticised only if they are based on modernity. According to statistical material, ethnic minorities are not being discriminated against in higher education. In a 260-page government report, however, the discrimination of ethnic minorities in higher education is subject to sharp critique. All of these arguments are based on emotions. It is not about the merits of an argument; whether, for instance, it is right or wrong to break with one's culture. It is about moralism, about populism with no scientific concern whatsoever – certain things are undermined and others are boosted.

Seven. While ethnic minorities are being drenched in mythology, any similar tendency is out of the question regarding one's own tradition. 'They' are fascinating. 'We' are uninteresting. 'They' are enriching, and renew our organisations – 'we' do not. 'They are vital to the future of Sweden'. 'Their' domestic affairs are vibrant, 'ours' frankly a bore. Dancing dervishes are incredible, and Swedish folk dance is right-wing. Nationalism is scrutinised while diversity – simultaneously – is overflowing with nationalist verbiage. As opposed to extreme right-wing tiresome opposition to all things unknown and praise for the domestic, all hostility against the stranger is, in *Diversity at the University*, described as the product of an overheated imagination and *never* as the result of an insecure social reality. Worth repeating, George Orwell referred to this as 'negative nationalism', i.e. a self-obsession identical to old-school nationalism save for the fact that one's own country is no longer hailed but dragged through the mire. The passage also captures the essence of Orwell's 'transferred nationalism' – the same nationalism, only not here but over there.

Emerging from these paragraphs – a streak of authoritarianism, a surreptitious racism, a foretaste of reactionary and animalistic thought, of myths of ethnicity, pseudo-radicalism, essentialism, and a rhetoric filled with moralism and emotions – is the edifice of conservatism, the ideology of the privileged and the insider. The building blocks of the report came out on the losing end of the battle against modernity. The enemy is chiselled out: human rights, the rights of the individual, a secular state, the Enlightenment, open discussion, and solidarity – a particular kind of respect cutting through groups, the ethnic group among them. An abyss separates diversity and modernity.

Diversity plans at eight universities

This study of multiculturalism in the West has been based on the Swedish university as a case study. According to *Diversity at the University* – one of the most extensive multicultural documents in Sweden – multiculturalism has a conservative tendency. Apart from a generous attitude towards immigrants, not much is left of its progressive ambitions.

Now we shall turn to the fact that the report had commissioned the universities to give multiculturalism status as an underlying norm. The question is: how did the universities respond? Was their reaction a reminder of academic independence? The halls of learning were, indeed, the proper place for well-rounded criticism. Or, in a time of underfinanced heavy expansion, was all of this set aside for the benefit of submissiveness and pragmatism?

As earlier noted, *Diversity at the University* had recommended that the social democratic government earmark two and a half billion Swedish Kronor in total over the initial five years for the universities' diversity work – and then 'assess whether financial resources shall vary according to success in multicultural ambitions'.[318] Was this an offer they could refuse?

In order to find an answer to these questions, the so-called diversity plans will be studied. These documents were the result of being commissioned by the social democratic government. The material used is made up by diversity plans at eight of the largest universities and university colleges in Sweden: Stockholm University; Göteborg University, Uppsala University, Umeå University, Linköping University, The University of Linné, and Malmö Högskola – Sweden's largest university college.[319] This second part of the book is a national survey of diversity plans at the Swedish University. In addition, other sources will illuminate the discussion, such as course plans and seminar adverts. Initially, these diversity plans will be briefly presented. Then follows how they are being legitimised, along with a critical assessment thereof. Subsequently, we shall turn to a critical analysis. The ambition is only to present an overview and make a few introductory comments. As in *Diversity at the university*, we are dealing with diversity in the sense of ethnic diversity.

Stockholm University

'The quest for active diversity work rests ultimately on the shoulders of the Director at Stockholm University'.[320] Responsible for active diversity work on the level of faculty and department are 'The Dean, chief administrators, department administration managers, The Head Librarian, and Prefects' and others in a similar position.[321]

'The Human Resources Office' and 'The office of student affairs' are operationally responsible for diversity work at Stockholm University.[322] Office of Staff is responsible for the mapping of 'measures implemented in order to increase diversity among staff'[323] Diversity work at Stockholm University is to be 'conducted in multiple phases and shall be founded on work-place experience'.[324] Every measure shall be carried through without any group or individual feeling addressed and embarrassed.[325] Assigned faculties and Office of Staff are responsible for finding tools in order to continuously assess diversity work. Each and every head is furthermore responsible for 'fostering (...) diversity in his/her unit as well as prevent problems that may arise (...) between staff members and students as a result of different backgrounds'.[326]. Efforts to foster diversity are to be highlighted 'in the action plan for environment at work' – produced on a yearly basis by each department.[327]

Uppsala University

Fostering diversity, it is claimed at Uppsala University, is 'a continuous and strategic undertaking, implying that a great deal of activities must be simultaneously conducted within various parts of the organization.'[328] The Director of the university 'has the overarching responsibility to assure that Uppsala University is actively engaged in goal-oriented diversity work'.[329] At this point, the goals of the university are seen as of supreme importance. In order for these goals to be fulfilled 'measures are required on all levels of the organisation'.[330] The head in charge is to 'support diversity in his/her own field of expertise in order to foster a creative work environment'.[331] 'Those operatively responsible for work with diversity issues in this plan are indicated under each intervention'.[332]

Among tasks assigned to the *Committee for Ethnic and Social Diversity* is fostering of ethnic diversity among students and employees, and – 'in connection to various supplementary courses' – suggesting how 'diversity-related questions might be stressed during information meetings'.[333]

The goal in Diversity plan 2007–2009 is to ensure that diversity work 'shall be part of the internal work of the departments'.[334] The head of human resources is to ensure that the diversity aspect is taken into consideration 'at audit of the personnel political program.'[335] 'The head of personnel along with head of the international office are to ensure that employees and student representatives are being informed about our discrimination laws and about our law on equal treatment of students'.[336] The university is entitled to distribute its manual entitled *On Ethnic and Related Discrimination.* Responsible: Head of personnel and Head of the Dept. of Law.[337] The development of a new diversity plan falls upon the Prefect at the Dept. of Nordic Languages and Head of Student Office.[338] The task of offering support to the head of student office and human resources in order to follow up measures in the diversity plan falls upon the work group for the development of a diversity plan.[339] The work group for the development of a diversity plan was to ensure that a diversity calendar would be as widely read as in 2007 and 2008.[340]

Lund University

The Director of the university has the overarching responsibility for 'active diversity work' at Lund University, and each head has 'the daily responsibility to foster diversity within his/her department.'[341] Diversity is to be 'naturally ingrained' in personal planning, in tasks related to the work environment and it shall be 'focused when action plans are being finalised'.[342] Section Personnel are commissioned to follow up and present 'how the various areas of their diversity work is being transformed into action within the organisation', at the same time as head of human resources is 'operationally responsible for the conducting of goal-focused work, including offering continuous reports to the Director of the University'.[343] At Lund University, an advisory board shall assist the head of human resources. The task of this board is to 'suggest paths of future development in trying to foster equal rights and opportunities irrespective of ethnicity, religion, or other belief, and also to suggest how questions of diversity shall be addressed at the university'.[344]

The departments' yearly planning are stressed at the university, because this is where 'continuous efforts to implement and launch strategic and goal-focused diversity work' comes to the fore.[345] These annual plans aside, 'a follow-up of concrete measures' is being presented 'in reports and drafts presented along with the annual report'.[346] At this point, a process diary should be mentioned, in which the advisory board takes notes. In these notes 'pursued activities are taken down and measures are suggested in order to enhance continuous development work aiming to foster equal rights and opportunities at work'.[347] Lund University is 'actively' engaged in diversity work, and can offer a diversity plan for employees as well as an action plan to broaden student recruitment from among other ethnic minority groups.[348]

Umeå University

At Umeå University, the key responsibility for 'an inclusive university' is held by the Director, and 'each and every student and employee is expected to participate in the creation of an inclusive university'.[349] One of the goals is to increase 'knowledge among heads and leaders about the work aimed to foster diversity'.[350] Offering open seminars for heads and other leaders are mentioned among 'activities' to achieve this goal. (Responsible: Chairperson at the Board of Equal Treatment.); and, 'under the supervision of head of the unit for the training of personnel and organisation', it is to be ensured that 'aspects and diversity and equal treatment (shall) be conducted and further implemented (in) the core leadership programs of the university – short "UCL"'.[351]

The university stresses the importance of 'meeting the competence of the future and recruiting the most qualified students and employees'. It is therefore important, states the University, to broaden 'its base of recruitment' – in other words to 'increase diversity'.[352] In admissions and recruitment, the university shall 'consider the diversity aspect in the production of recruitment materials and in the planning and carrying through of recruitment campaigns'. This work is being done 'continuously', and the responsibility falls upon the head of information.[353] Concerning the employed, 'the chairperson of the Board of Equal Treatment is responsible for a continuous order of statistical material from "Statistics Sweden" concerning the division of employees with respect to foreign background in order to analyse and compare earlier statistical materials'.[354] During welcome ceremonies, the head of information – in liaison with the head of students, is in charge of efforts to inform about diversity work at Umeå University.[355] Deans and leaders are offered 'a dialogue (…) with the Board of Equal Treatment regarding their work in equal treatment and diversity related issues' in order to ensure that this information has been well received.[356] The assistant management director is furthermore to ensure that that none of the university's policy documents 'run counter to an inclusive attitude' and to diversity.[357] Under the responsibility of the chairperson of the Board of Equal Treatment, the university, as a part in an elaborate assessment policy, is to 'assemble what has been produced within the field of diversity on every single Faculty and Department'.[358] Regarding 'internationalisation', finally, the aim is to increase 'cooperation and exchange of ideas in work with internationalisation, diversity, and equality at the university'.[359] Two activities are singled out: The Board of Equal Treatment and the Committee for Internationalisation are commissioned to continuously carry out common activities for students and employees. Chairperson of the Board of Equal Treatment along with Chairperson for the Committee for Internationalisation is responsible for this. Chairperson for the Board of Equal Treatment along with the Committee for Internationalisation are jointly responsible for the finalising and assessing how Faculties and Departments have managed to make use of diversity in Swedish society in their efforts to enhance internationalisation.[360]

The University of Linné

Formally, the University of Linné no longer has any diversity plan. Instead, *Equality Plan for the University of Linné 2011 – concerning sexually transgressing identity or expression, ethnic belonging, religion or other faith, sexual predisposition or age* is being presented, replacing earlier diversity plans.[361] In the university's strategy for 2010-2015 entitled, *A journey into the future*, 'Global values, such as internationalisation, diversity' are said to pervade 'research, education and administrative functions at the University of Linné'.[362] In 'General prioritisation' under the university's 'Action Plan 2011–2014', emphasis on the concept of equality, it should be noted, remains strong: 'During the coming 3-year period, the emphasis on equality work will be characterised by increasing possibilities for systematic and goal-focused equality work'. There is, moreover, a desire to 'increase knowledge and awareness, among employees as well as among students, about the inherent worth of equality'.[363]

Despite this shift in perspective, references to diversity still exist, as in a case where equality and ethnic diversity is being combined: 'During personnel planning in Departments and courses, aspects of equality shall always be taken into consideration, and active recruiting efforts shall be conducted in order to foster ethnic diversity'.[364] The university offers a course entitled 'personal treatment of heterogeneous student groups'. 'Lecturers, administrative personnel, and others who communicate with students' constitute the target group.[365] In spite of the plan's relative brevity, it harbours an extensive supplement with definitions. In it, 'ethnic belonging' is, among other things defined as 'an individual's national and ethnic origin, skin colour, or related circumstance'. It is, the plan continues, the individual him/herself who defines his/her ethnic background and 'ethnic belonging relies on self-identification'.[366]

Malmö University College

At Malmö University College, diversity work permeates the entire organisation. The Director has the 'overarching responsibility to (...) ensure active and goal focused (...) diversity work'.[367] While section heads and unit heads are directly responsible for the execution of 'overarching (...) Diversity work', planning of 'overarching equality- and diversity work takes place in the central board for equality and diversity'.[368] At Malmö University College, everyone in a leading position advocates diversity because they all 'have knowledge, understanding and insight into legislation pertaining to (...) diversity and adhere to this policy as to other established documents in the area'.[369] The following citation shows that questions of diversity permeate the entire organisation from the top down: 'Issues of diversity remain an important part of collaboration at work related meetings, during performance reviews, on the management team, and during conversations in staff room'.[370] Perspectives of diversity are furthermore part of 'staff queries regarding for instance work conditions, work environment, recruitment, pay, and training, in questions related to maintenance and leadership, ultimately relating to the meeting with students, partners and citizens'.[371]

At Malmö University College, diversity related issues are already a remarkable success, since 'diversity is being included in every single issue and is on the agenda in all forms of collaborations'.[372] Locally as well as centrally, diversity is constantly in focus: in the work of local groups of collaboration, the overarching goal for diversity at the Malmö University college is being integrated at the same time as work conducted 'in the central group for equality and diversity (...) is being integrated and followed-up in the central group of collaboration'.[373] During recruitment, a profile of demands is done in order to foster diversity. The Central Board of Equality and Diversity is commissioned by the Director to conduct a comprehensive evaluation, forming the structure for an assessment based on the goals set by the activities along with the guiding rules and plans of actions. The assessment is conducted on two different levels – on the level of Malmö University College in general, and locally in each Department. In order to fuse vision and practice, area-specific diversity actions plans will be concretised based on 'general and long-term goals'[374]

Linköping University

The most recent plan at Linköping University relating to the questions at hand is no longer called a diversity plan, but the 'Strategy and Action Plan for Equal Opportunities 2012'. The plan of 2003 was, however, labelled a 'diversity plan', indicating a certain shift in meaning.[375]

'Responsibility for the task of the university to conduct goal-focused work within the area of equal opportunity' falls, it is stated under 'Division of responsibility', on the Director.[376] The message in 'Strategy and Action Plan for Equal Opportunities 2012' can be illustrated by the cover featuring a cartoon girl in a multi-colour striped T-shirt. Smiling wryly, legs apart, in dark glasses, she holds a pitbull on a short leash. Behind her a hammer stands in front of three nails and one screw. 'I treat everyone alike', says the hammer.[377]

In order 'to achieve the goal of "equal opportunity", (University of Linköping) fosters equality and gender, ethnic, and religious diversity, accessibility and participation for mentally challenged individuals, along with equal treatment irrespective of age or transgender identity/expression'.[378] The university, states the plan, rests on 'democratic basic values founded on human rights'.[379] We shall furthermore 'protect critical thinking which implies the right to express your views even though these might be considered unpleasant by some'.[380] Then again, it is 'important to stress the fact that particular employees or students might feel humiliated when other employees or students make use of their freedom of speech. The risk of conflicting views', the plan continues, 'is particularly pronounced when the topic at hand is religion or other forms of confession'.[381]

Linköping University, the plan states, is 'a non-confessional university based on a scientific worldview.'[382] Then again, a prayer room is available.[383] The university is adamant that ethnic variety should flourish. Therefore, 'by means of strategic and preventative efforts', 'one endeavours to profit from ethnic diversity and retain the rights of the individual to choose various religions and faiths'.[384] At the university, various seminars and initiatives are being conducted aiming to 'increase cultural understanding'.[385] A multi-religious calendar has, as an example, been distributed to every student union, departments, and units in order to increase awareness at work about various religious holidays. 'Goal: to create a work and study environment where everybody feels welcome'.[386] In spring 2012 ten lectures were held in order to increase awareness about honour structures.[387]

Göteborg University

The Director at Göteborg University has 'the final responsibility to ensure that laws and regulations concerning equal treatment are being defended'. At the level of departments and faculties, this task falls upon deans, the registrar, and heads of departments or people in similar positions.[388] Increased diversity throughout the entire organisation contributes to 'higher quality throughout'.[389] Göteborg University is in the process of constant change and flux in order to assure a good work environment where all the employed and all students irrespective (…) of ethnicity, religion or other faith (…) are allowed to flourish'.[390] 'Prevent and oppose harassment' is stated among 'general goals for equal treatment'.[391] Competent applicants who show 'another cultural/language background than the one displayed by the majority of employees are recommended to apply (…) for "vacancies at the university"'.[392]

Educational activities within diversity

Apart from these measures, the eight universities and university colleges above are also engaged in comprehensive educational activities within the field of diversity – internal as well as on behalf of the students. At Stockholm University, leaders are singled out for special education in diversity, and lectures and seminars in issues related to diversity are being arranged throughout the university.[393] Students are, for instance, offered a course titled 'Ethnicity, diversity and integration', and a master's program in 'intersectionality studies – i.e. the study of collaboration in between various societal categorisations of human beings, according to which special treatment may occur, such as (…) ethnicity'.[394]

The head of department for educational development at Uppsala University is commissioned to 'educate personnel and course representatives in up-to-date jurisdiction' concerning diversity.[395] In the coming period 'new research projects concerning diversity at Uppsala University will be initiated', and 'preconditions in order to carry through an investigation about plausible ethno-, or socially-based biased recruitment at the research level will be subject to examination'.[396] The Committee for Ethnic and Social Diversity shall 'initiate diversity perspectives in the undergraduate course in Education for teachers' as well as 'arrange seminars to foster knowledge about ethnic (...) diversity.' At Uppsala University, a course is offered entitled 'the Paradoxes of Diversity', focusing on 'ethnicity and diversity in order to problematise central concepts and discuss experiences for various societies'. This course has not only students in mind: 'Those who work at the university are also encouraged to take the course'.[397]

At Lund University, students are offered an undergraduate program in the development of diversity. The program – entitled *Equality and Diversity Management* – 'teaches how to foster and spread diversity, service and development at work'.[398] To those in a leading position – safety controllers, and diversity contact persons, seminars and education will be carried out.[399]

Malmö University College offers students a great variety of courses and programs in diversity. As an example, each and every field at the Program for Social Work has a diversity profile.[400] The reason why diversity has such a dominant position at Malmö University College is partly related to a long-standing ambition whereby 'key areas of perspectives' – such as Ethnic Relations – shall permeate 'all education, research, and all other activity'.[401] The knowledge section entitled IMER – *International Migration and Ethnic Relations* – is important to the College's self-perception, and it is moreover, according to its Program description 'plain to see' that 'the most advanced society of today (...) has been constructed by groups of immigrants'.[402] As a consequence, concepts such as integration, segregation, assimilation, multiculture, diversity, discrimination and racism are addressed throughout the University

College. Another important reason as to why diversity is a focus relates to the fact that Malmö University College especially caters to groups unfamiliar with academic studies, such as students with an immigrant background. The ideology of diversity, it is hoped, will have a positive influence on these students. At *The University of Linné*, a course is offered entitled 'the treatment of heterogeneous students groups', aimed at teachers, administrators, and others who in their daily work interact with students.[403]

How is the ideology of diversity legitimised?

The above outline is meant only to summarise how diversity is being laid out in the various plans. These questions will be systematically discussed at this time. The analysis is limited to two key themes; legitimising and criticising diversity. In Chapter 9, 'How is the ideology of diversity being legitimised?' – a few aspects central to diversity will be subject to critical examination. In Chapter 10, 'Six cases of criticism', a number of more general weaknesses in the ideology of diversity will be brought to attention.

Diversity as self-evident

Slightly simplified, one may defend an argument in social sciences in two different ways. Either this is done by debate, or the argument is seen as 'self-evident'. Either the subjectivity of the presentation is recognised, leading to a scientific and sceptical analysis, or the subjectivity is not recognised, ending in an emotionally charged and dogmatic argument. The first alternative rests on the ideas of the Enlightenment, while the second one is rooted in an anti-intellectual tradition. When things were seen as 'evident', this created tranquillity among the population, and the importance of this must not be underestimated. Still, we are witnessing an authoritarian exercise of power banning all discussion and stifling social change. The philosophy of the Enlightenment – followed by Marxists and liberals, challenged these reactionary ideas. Undeniably, they had the right to exist, but only as one perspective among many others. This was, in other words, an *ideology*. This development in societal maturity, when traditionalism pressed by modernity and relativism gradually was replaced by a self-conscious conservatism and ideology has been thoroughly discussed by the German sociologist Karl Mannheim.[404]

How, then, does the rhetoric of diversity fit into this scheme? Here are a few examples. At Lund University, in planning of personnel and when the work environment is discussed, 'diversity', it is stated, 'shall be a *natural component that* must be addressed when action plans are laid out'.[405] 'Issues of diversity', according to the former Director of Malmö University College, are to be '*naturally integrated* throughout our organisation'.[406] In the diversity plan at Malmö University College, 'the perspective of diversity seems to be a *self-evident* aspect in training for leadership, and in staff supplementary courses'.[407]

At Lund University, students are offered an undergraduate program in diversity development. The program – entitled *Equality and Diversity Management* – teaches the students 'how to work with diversity (...) and development at the modern workplaces of today'.[408] The diversity plan at Uppsala University announces that department heads shall 'foster diversity within their area of responsibility, *which in turn* will generate a creative work environment'.[409] Issues of diversity, the diversity plan at Malmö University College states, are 'a factor for competition and success at departmental level and also to Malmö University College'.[410] In their ambitious diversity plan, Lund University claims to carry out open seminars on diversity issues for employees in order to foster an open university where *diversity is being recognised and is allowed to enrich the entire organisation'*.[411] (My italics.)

The then Director of Malmö University College states: 'It is my conviction that our educations and our activities will be better off and more *thoroughly reflected* if we actively make use of the diversity of experiences carried by our students and our employees'.[412] In the plan for equal treatment at Göteborg University, it says that 'increased diversity among students and staff members leads to "*higher quality* in the organization"', and in the diversity plan at Stockholm University, it is claimed that 'we shall continue to develop diversity among staff members'.[413] Everyone seems to agree that diversity contributes to 'development', to 'higher quality', to a more 'thoroughly reflected' organisation, to a 'creative work environment' and that diversity constitutes 'a factor for competition and success'. 'Diversity enriches the entire organisation'. Diversity is 'natural'. Diversity is 'obvious'.

The above citations share the fact that diversity is not being questioned. The tone is enthusiastic, and the line of argument is emotional. But why not focus instead on other concepts such as solidarity or citizenship? Diversity is ideology in thin disguise. The theory of diversity poses many important questions and should have its protagonists at the university. Still, the perspective of diversity must be challenged by other perspectives – liberal, Marxist, republican and so on. Diversity is neither natural nor self-evident. Nobody would suggest that Swedish universities should be saturated by Max Weber's ideal types. Then why is diversity accepted with no questions asked?

Diversity as natural science

A similar way to legitimise these diversity plans is to use metaphors from the natural sciences. The advisory board for diversity issues at Lund University was commissioned to 'suggest how the university should *make visible* questions of diversity'.[414] When you *make visible* you make known what is already there. When diversity is *made visible*, the categorisations relating to diversity are assigned the same dignity as those pertaining to natural science. You can, on the other hand, never make liberalism visible because the principles of liberalism are open to discussion. Whether you 'make visible', 'uncover', or 'map', diversity is given a natural scientific authority it simply does not have.

This natural scientific enthusiasm creates confusion when you are getting a taste of your own medicine. In 2008, the newspaper *Fokus* presented a so-called 'diversity-ranking', where Swedish universities and university colleges were listed based on the extent they could fulfil 'the political goals of society'. The University of Södertörn ranked No1 in the category 'number of students with foreign background'.[415] The student newspaper *Lundagård* recently commented on the fact that Lund University for years has been actively engaged in trying to increase the number of foreign students, but still, according to the 2008 report, ranks at 'rock bottom'. 'We don't know why', Lund University answers with some consternation, while the administrators at Södertörn University College smile.[416]

But what is this really about? It is not about something that is to be uncovered but, which is also openly recognised, about *political goals*, i.e. about *ideology*. It is easy to come out on top of *Fokus*'s width-ranking. All you have to do is to bar applications from people with Swedish roots. This kind of measure is, moreover, rather insecure. Perhaps Lund University had without success dedicated both time and energy to the question, while Södertörn University College was only by accident located in an area with a large proportion of immigrants.

Diversity as information

Another way to legitimise the ideology of diversity is to reduce it to a matter of 'information'. Staff members at the university might, for instance, be invited to 'information meetings' where the benefits of diversity are explained. It is one thing to inform children. They know little, and need to be informed and adults teach children – fair enough. But according to the advocates of diversity, adults also need to be informed and made aware. Uppsala University has a committee for ethnic and social diversity. Its task it to 'suggest forms for how questions of increased diversity can be emphasised during information seminars and programs for personnel and students'.[417] In the diversity plan at Malmö University College 'active and goal-oriented work is conducted where students and members of staff are offered information and method assistance about the benefits of diversity.'[418] The diversity plan at Stockholm University emphasises 'education and information', and seeks to 'affect attitudes and raise awareness'.[419] The diversity plan at Lund University tries to achieve 'enhanced information and communication' with staff members, and leaders are to push forward in these efforts in order to create an 'open and inclusive' work environment.[420] Diversity is, however, only one ideology among many. All you say or 'write has political implications, even if you explicitly choose to avoid to take sides' or dress it up in neutral terminology.[421] The hidden statement behind any form of 'communication' or 'information' about the virtues of diversity is this: Our ideology is right and yours is wrong. This is the same thing as if a Marxist is obliged to become a liberal, or a liberal to convert to Catholicism.

The problem relating to diversity at the university is not that dissenters are uninformed. Surely, we are informed. We have not become unconscious and need to be woken up. We have only reached other conclusions. When I was working in Stockholm there were always a few members of the Jehovah Witnesses at the local train station in Flemingsberg selling their periodical *Wake Up!* One early morning I went up to one of them and said: 'I am awake'.

In short, the thought that only the enthusiast understands is a sectarian and religious thought. Those who have read Alexander Solzhenitsyn, George Orwell, or Primo Levi know that this is the way political extremism works. It is the backbone of any form of totalitarian thinking. One important thought at the emerging universities many centuries ago was that critique, too, could be based on knowledge. All rhetoric about being 'aware', 'open', and having to be 'awakened' or be led to 'insight' shows that normal arguments are no longer needed.[422] In this new situation, the directive document of the organisations is something that 'at best must be accepted by the grassroots'. Real 'political alternatives have been replaced by the practice of rational order – an ideology itself bearing the witness of absolute control.'[423] The heads at Lund University, worth noting, are told to 'push forward' – a metaphor from cattle breeding. The expression is honest in its unabashed brutality.

This way of reasoning also comes in a different form that only appears less ruthless. When a political party loses voters, the comments appear to be a kind of self-criticism: 'We have failed to reach out'. Still, perhaps you have, and therefore nobody votes for you. The ideology of diversity is defended along similar lines. 'Our information campaigns have been insufficient'. 'We have failed to reach out'. 'We are to blame for this'. But why, really, are they to blame? Because others still insist that diversity is a bad thing. We are humble and bow graciously because you do not share our views, and we promise to do better so that you will soon share our views.

As a part in these information campaigns, we are offered methodological support. We embrace diversity not because we are motivated by good arguments or forced to but because were are given assistance and guidance. It might seem caring, but may also indicate a power so hegemonic it does not even have to resort to violence. This interpretation is not far-fetched because all intellectual independence has been taken away. Instead the dissident is seen as unwell and mentally unstable. Why this is associated with 'diversity' is not quite clear. *Xinhua* – the Chinese state broadcaster – recently announced that a number of individuals had been 'corrected and educated'.[424] Political parallels should be used with caution. Yet, even in Sweden, the dissident may be diagnosed as unaware. Suppose you would arrange a seminar about the drawbacks of diversity. Offer support and education.

Diversity as internationalisation

The diversity plans contain numerous references to internationalisation. In their diversity plan, you can read 'Uppsala University is an international work environment where creativity is enriched by diversity. International influence has been quite central ever since its initiation'.[425] And further on: 'Uppsala University shall become an international workplace with a multicultural character'.[426] Lund University, their diversity plan claims, shall 'strive to foster ethnic and international diversity in our academic environment'.[427] It is maintained, 'International contacts and a free exchange of ideas across borders have been crucial in research development'. Universities are also defended generally: 'The need for educated people and competitive research is greater than ever before'.[428] Having stated that diversity shall 'characterise the work environment' at Stockholm University, the plan claims 'the university has (...) always been guided by an open and international perspective, and that a 'free and open atmosphere is a crucial precondition for the development of the organisation'.[429] 'Activities within the framework of internationalisation are', the Strategy Plan of Linköping university declares, 'expected to contribute to an increased international exchange of students as well as staff and to an increased understanding for cultural differences and equalities'. 'The work for equal opportunities', it is added, 'benefits from this'.[430] In the Strategy Plan at the University of Linné 2010-2015, it is stated that 'global values' such as internationalisation and diversity shall permeate all research, education and administrative functions at the University of Linné'.[431]

According to the universities, international exchange, such as studies abroad and researcher exchanges, is something good and popular and the universities are keen to associate diversity with it. Diversity and international exchange are, however, two different things. Internationalisation is about the shrinking importance of the nation state, increased mobility across borders, and politically and ideologically it is intimately connected to globalisation. As a political idea, the ideology of diversity maintains that the university should be constructed according to collectivist – notably ethnic and religious – criteria, where borders between groups are to be protected in order to shield their respective interest and identities. Internationalisation is about the tearing down of all demarcation lines, while the diversity nervously wants to prevent them. Diversity is a discourse about the inherent worth of difference – internationalisation is all about standardisation and equality. You cannot call it diversity just because researchers come to Sweden or our students go abroad. The diversity plan at Lund University refers to 'international diversity'.[432] The scientific weight of the concept is not strengthened by the fact that a Google search can only find it in a Swedish church local community instruction and on the website of Karlstad folk high school west of Stockholm.[433]

The above arguments are also elusive at times. Stockholm University, characterised by diversity, is seamlessly allowed to slide over to the following statement: 'Stockholm University was always characterised by an international perspective'.[434] Most likely, anyone who advocates for diversity is also expected to have a broad perspective that, in turn, might explain why criticism against diversity is seen as nationalism, and nationalism is, as we all know, tantamount to right-wing extremism. Here, too, the association between diversity and international exchange fails to convince.

As such, internationalisation is an enthusiastic and aggressive project – diversity is sentimental. The following statement is also somewhat troublesome: 'International contacts and a free exchange of ideas across borders have been crucial for the development of research'.[435] It should be noted that this citation occurs in a diversity plan with the explicit purpose of giving credibility to this ideology. But exactly why should a free exchange of views be preconditioned by diversity? And why speak about a 'free exchange of ideas' when the discourse of diversity has merged with the state and all critique is labelled right-wing radical? The advocates of diversity are not inclined to question their own views. Instead, intellectual insecurity is replaced by a kind of authoritative emotionalism. This 'ever more fragile ability to self-criticism', Christopher Lasch comments, 'is the safest sign of the pending death of an intellectual tradition'.[436]

The need for 'highly educated people and competitive research', the plan at Lund University stresses, 'is more urgent than ever before'.[437] There are two ways to read this. Either it is seen as standing on its own, which makes it true but trivial. Or, a more likely interpretation, it is linked to diversity. But why should the idea of diversity – one political idea among many others – be associated with successful research? Internationalisation bursts open all borders, among them the walls of ethnicity. Competitive research does not presuppose human beings being divided into collective identities. Exchange of ideas is not necessarily aided by the fact that the state nods in approval.

Regarding the *Strategy and action plan for equal opportunities* at Linköping University, this plan, as indicated by its name, is no longer chiefly linked to diversity. Instead it focuses on an opposite discourse of equal opportunities. Yet there are many examples whereby diversity remains strong and the conflict with progressive equal opportunity is agonisingly clear. The work towards increasing international exchanges, the above citation claims, leads to an 'increased understanding for cultural (...) differences', which in turn 'benefits the work for equal opportunity'.[438] The link between international exchange and diversity does not convince. Having international contacts does not mean that we are excited about our differences, but about how science brings us together. Moreover: why should endeavours for 'equal opportunities' benefit from an 'understanding of cultural differences'. We have to choose. Either we sink our soul in the inequality, in the difference, the local, the particular, the cultural; in the abyss and the division, in the distinctive, dissenting, incomprehensible, odd, and contradictory. Or, we choose to defend commonalities that unite us: scientific principles and standards and our 'shared conditions' as individuals, citizens, and human beings. You can choose relativism or universalism, but not both at the same time. Why create equality – legal, social political or economical – with those you sense are distant? The idea that understanding and proximity is like the Phoenix born out of the ashes of alienation and distance is one the left's more break necking utopias.

Diversity as social engineering

This chapter showed that diversity is legitimised by being presented as something self-evident (which it is not), as natural science (which it is not), as a mere case of information (which it is not), and as closely linked to internationalisation (which it is not). Apparently, it is being defended through a lot of disparate qualities, and the impression is altogether confusing.

This leads into postmodernity; perceived as creative by its protagonists, and as contradictory by its critics. Diversity may be associated with postmodernity – in the defence of the minority and difference, in the critique against 'the norm', and in the penchant for ethnic and other categorisations. But the ideology of diversity also seeks to win acceptance by borrowing ideas from modernity – not the least from the thought of social engineering and the idea of the new human.

For instance, this comes to the fore in its attitude towards discrimination. 'Not being discriminated against is', says the diversity plan at Stockholm University, 'a human right', and 'it is a central aspect in the work for a positive psycho-social work environment'.[439] 'Irrespective (...) of ethnic background, faith, disability or age, everybody', says the plan for Malmö University College, 'has the same possibilities for employment, along with development, influence and promotion in his/her occupation'.[440] Lund University's diversity document states, 'we have zero tolerance for discriminatory special treatment'.[441] By all means, a work place is better if people are friendly. But why should 'not being discriminated against' be declared a 'human right'? Unless declarations such as this have some kind of relation to the world we are living in, they are merely words on paper.

Is age not an issue when you look for a job? Would a sixty-year old with no higher education expect the same promotion possibilities as a young researcher? Merely claiming that a person with mental difficulties can climb in his/her career at the same rate as someone fortunate enough to be born healthy is not humane but grotesque. This statement bears witness of a kind of equality and optimism where all relation to our unjust reality has gone missing – in other words social engineering at its most offensive; an enthusiasm gone monstrous.

Zero tolerance to discrimination is no less strange because 'to think in absolute terms is not to think at all'.[442] In addition, they want to control your thoughts. Why is not a college allowed to dislike me? Are our private emotions the business of the university? In case this is a place of freedom of thought, does this not, then, entail a mild case of constricted animosity? 'Sexual harassment or any other form of harassment', we are told, 'does not exist at Malmö University College'.[443] How come they know this? Is it true?

At a Moscow writers' conference, having overheard endless speeches of universal happiness, André Malraux asked: 'And what about the child being overrun by a tram?' Following an embarrassing silence someone said in a storm of applauds: 'In a flawless, planned socialist traffic system, no accident ever happens'.[444] The enthusiasm of diversity and multiculturalism is set on a course from humanism and tolerance towards totalitarianism.

When they are engaged 'against racism and xenophobia', the classic idea whereby universities are silent and researchers speak has been lost. Who can possibly guarantee that the tables are not suddenly turned, and we instead are howling 'in favour or racism and xenophobia'? Institutions serving as moral megaphones are better suited in authoritarian systems, and emotions are notoriously unreliable as they tend to swing from one extreme to another. The fact that our universities defend 'good values' against 'bad values' is a bleak excuse because *all* politicians are convinced that their opinions are good – Hitler included. Marching for anti-racism is not the logical alternative to racism. The logical alternative is doing nothing at all.

Diversity as anti-racism

We have already touched upon diversity's intricate relation to racism (and to anti-racism). A few comments will be made linked to the plans above. In order to seek legitimacy via anti-racism, the critique against diversity is deemed as politically suspect, often as racist. Thus, diversity at the university is given an aura of moral righteousness.

But diversity is no more than one ideology among many. As such it may be questioned from many perspectives which are neither right-wing extremist nor racist. Diversity may, for instance, be criticised by means of objectivism and critical thinking, against its tendencies towards self-righteousness and relativism. It may be scrutinised by universalism, because diversity is founded upon group rights – putting the partial interest ahead of the general interest. The rhetoric of diversity can be held accountable through classic leftist critiques such as egalitarianism and equality. Why is that? Because the rhetoric sides with difference and inequality. It may be scrutinized by means of solidarity irrespective of class and other social distinctions, because the idea of diversity is potentially disintegrating – i.e. it threatens to dissolve every tendency towards *transcultural* understanding for the benefit of sectarianism and a black-and-white division between 'us' and 'them'. It may moreover be criticised from a Marxist perspective because the concept of class triumphs over any other social category, ethnicity among them. While a person with ethnic background may well belong to the upper class, a person from the lower class – by definition – cannot. This is the reason why the concept of class is so powerful. As opposed to the waterproof concept of class, ethnicity has holes in it left and right. Sweden has numerous immigrant politicians, but if a person who sleeps rough is a politician, he/she is no longer sleeping rough. Diversity's liberal reputation may also be questioned, since the entire ideology has mythical/collectivist traits where our individuality is pushed aside for the benefit of ethnic background.

The above arguments are about the criticism against diversity – a criticism that is not necessarily racist. We may also ask questions of diversity's own active anti-racism. In the Equality plan at the University of Linné, ethnic belonging is 'according to the law any individual's national and ethnic background, skin colour, or similar condition'. The law cited is *Diskrimineringslagen* (2008:567) (The law against discrimination), where 'Ethnic belonging' under Ch. 1, § 5:3 is defined as 'national or ethnic origin, skin colour or other similar condition'.[445] Ethnic belonging is, hence, defined according to skin colour. Why is that? Because the multicultural left wants to attack racism head-on, and this, it is argued, is best done if skin colour is introduced as a basis for definition on behalf of minority groups. Any liberal attitude suggesting that skin colour can be replaced by methodological individualism is seen as a suspect half-measure and almost worse than the very racism it purports to oppose. At this point, the multicultural left carries on a long tradition. During the period between the great wars, the Social Democrats were habitually seen as 'social fascists' because they did not share the view of the extreme left of how to attack fascism.

However, a correct angle from which to make use of biological racial categories – phrenological qualities such as the tip of the forehead, the width of the nose, the thickness of the lips, or skin colour – does not exist. Whether you make use of it on behalf of Aryans or for the sake of ethnic minorities you are picking up political principles deemed poisonous ever since 1945 – at least outside the realm of the radical right. When we replace biologically founded aversion against the unknown with biologically founded idealisation, we are merely upturning the entire racist scheme. Either you oppose biologism and *the idea* that human beings may be classified based on the colour of their skin, or you claim that we can be defined according to skin colour – and pay the political prize. In case vicious biologism applies only when you say it does, you need to explain why this is so. Unless you do, you are only acting like the late 19th century imperialists once did: when 'we' violated law and order overseas, this could be justified because 'we' had the right to do it. When other cultures tried to defend themselves this was unacceptable, because 'they' had no right to do so. Now a mirror image emerges. The definition of ethnic belonging expressed at the University of Linné and in *Diskrimineringslagen* (the Law against discrimination), is not about political ideas but about who is be saluted and who is to be silenced. A political and scientific question is, thus, being brutalised to a moral issue of right and wrong. The social anthropologist Jonathan Friedman refers to this as a 'moralisation of the political'.[446]

In addition, this definition of ethnic belonging surpasses the academic discussion around ethnicity and nationalism. Neither the modernists Benedict Anderson, Ernest Gellner, nor for that matter Anthony Smith – who at times are attacked for being 'primordialist' – refer to skin colour or biology. Admittedly, Smith talks about 'ethnic cores' but this is not about biology but about culture and a shared world of symbolic expressions. The only ones who have defended ethnic belonging in terms of biology are the National Socialists, which does not quite strengthen the image of multiculturalism as being progressive.

For some time now, the multicultural left has been hegemonic. Instead of being criticised in open debates – so essential for all parties – it has been met with silence or nervous consent. The fact that a university and the Swedish law *against* discrimination embrace Nazi classifications is a good case in point. I assume that the number of people engaged in these matters must be counted by the hundreds. And yet – none of these university servants, officers, bureaucrats and academics have addressed this matter of fact: you cannot use skin colour against racism. When all critique is off-track, any hegemonic power will start justifying ever more outrageous views. Self-reflection evaporates and emotional euphoria is piling skyward. Critique against diversity is not always racism, and diversity is not always anti-racism.

Six cases of criticism

Previously we have discussed how the ideology of diversity and multiculturalism has been legitimised. Weaknesses have been addressed. Now we shall turn towards a more general critical discussion divided into six distinct themes. The first one deals with the definition of diversity, and the second one points at an internal contradiction between individual and collective. Number three and four focus on the concept of 'inequality' while number five distinguishes between ethnic 'presence' and 'ideas'. The sixth and final one presents a short overview of the international critique against the ideology of diversity.

Diversity – an attempt at a definition

The concept of diversity is being defended with great enthusiasm. It is therefore of interest to explore how it is being defined at the university. In this endeavour, the diversity plans are not of much avail. Instead, strong emotional sympathy is combined with only a vague understanding of what it really means. They are applauding into the dark.

And yet, attempts at a definition are made. In Supplement 1 in the diversity plan at Malmö University College – *Conceptual definitions* – the law against discrimination is called upon, and the supplement offers short definitions of concepts central to the discussion.[447] The most important concept in a diversity plan – the very concept of *diversity* – is, however, left out. The diversity plan at Stockholm University also contains definitions – again, however, without including a clarifying discussion about the meaning of diversity.[448]

Instead, the plans offer strongly positive value judgements with the sole purpose – it seems – to replace a scientifically rigorous analysis. In the plan at Linköping University, diversity is defined as a 'mixture of differences and equalities such as gender, age, sexual predisposition, ethnic background, religion or other faith, handicap or social background'. Regrettably, the precision then goes utterly missing: 'At Linköping university, the concept is about seeing, understanding, cherishing and profiting from this mix'.[449]

Oscillating between collective and individual

As in *Diversity at the University*, the diversity plans try to fuse the individual with the collective. The idea of diversity revolves around the idea of identity and homogeneity of the ethnic group, and the inherent worth of protecting this identity in an increasingly insecure and turbulent world. But the idea also entails that the ethnic representative who is assigned to speak on behalf of his (rarely 'her') group is swept into a mist of romanticism, in which political accountability is wiped aside for the benefit of 'shared roots' – an image seemingly more populist and right-wing extremist than democratically leftist.

The advocates of diversity overlook the fact that this collectivism is incongruent with individualism. The ideology of diversity and the liberal thought of the autonomous individual are, instead, proposed at one and the same time. Three examples will suffice. 'By means of strategic and pre-emptive measures', Linköping University's plan informs us, they 'strive to cater for ethnic diversity and also to respect the individual's right to have different religions and faiths'[450] The problem is only that – like any other collectivist theory – diversity replaces the rights of the individual with the rights of the collective. The entire bag of diversity – spokespersons, roots, culture, background, belonging, history, and identity (constantly based in the culture) – amply shows the secondary importance of the individual.

In its *Plan for Equal Treatment*, the University of Linné maintains that 'the individual herself defines her ethnic qualities, and that ethnic belonging rests on self-identification'.[451] This might all sound postmodern and elastic, and anybody should feel free to salute ethnicity and the individual at once. But who would seriously claim that ethnic belonging is the net result of 'self-identification'? The ethnic minority – on behalf of which diversity advocates struggle – would not do it. These groups – often squeezed between what is perceived as Western decadence and the religious and historical demands of their own culture – have no reason to be unclear. For them, ethnic concord is often of paramount importance. And what about the critical discussion about ethnic belonging? Again, the answer is no. Ethnic belonging is not about self-identification. To the contrary – the entire critique against ethnic belonging says that ethnicity *prohibits* self-identification and *prohibits* the individual – often women – from deciding how they should live.

Where, then, does this odd statement make sense? In the academic ivory towers of multiculturalism and postmodernity. Up here only, ethnicity is equipped with revolving doors. Here, Christopher Lasch says, 'in an artificial world where simulations of reality have replaced the real stuff, is multiculturalism about the free choice of the individual.[452] The multicultural entourage is eager to not appear as racists. As a result they fabricate arguments where ethnic minority groups are being humiliated.[453] Nobody wants to know what these people have to say.

'In each area of the commissariat', says the diversity plan at Uppsala University, 'members of staff and students shall be given the opportunity to partake in a seminar about the three-year-based strategic plans for equal opportunities, diversity, accessibility, equality, equal treatment and expanded recruitment'.[454] Yet again, diversity and equality are defended in the same breath. The idea of equality, going back to the idea of *egalité* of the French Revolution, is about the equal right of each and every human being. It is, thus, based on the individual. As I have previously tried to show, the idea of diversity is, in contrast, based on the collective. The ethnic *group* is in focus – *not* its distinct individuals. Even though party politics recently appear somewhat postmodern, a liberal is a liberal, and a communist is a communist. Yet again one gets the impression that the diversity plans make use of about anything with an appealing ring without wondering too much whether these ideas can be combined at all.

Then, you might say, this definition of diversity is still too narrow. Diversity, in fact, is far less ambitious, such as universities aspiring for general pluralism. But this definition is so all-embracing it no longer makes sense. Who would oppose academic pluralism?

If the idea of diversity it to be taken seriously, it rests on a number of premises such as the homogeneity of the ethnic group, mythologised identities and 'shared historical experience', all concepts in square opposition to liberal, progressive and egalitarian concepts such as equality and solidarity. Efforts to address the individual and the student in a diversity plan are futile.

These ethnic plans, moreover, appear to fuel rather than hinder ethnic stereotypes. The plan at Uppsala University tells us 'every applicant shall be evaluated according to her individual qualities irrespective of ethnic, social or religious belonging'.[455] At the University of Linné, it is claimed that all 'human beings have the same value irrespective of gender, nationality, ethnic origin or age'.[456] In the same spirit, Stockholm University informs us that they wish to 'create a work climate where all employees may prosper and cooperate irrespective of background'.[457] But why keep talking about ethnic background if it does not matter? Why are we being locked in inside distinct ethnic communities, only to then be requested to 'communicate across cultural borders'? Our background, Uppsala University says, is irrelevant. But why not leave us alone then?

Because, I assume, it is deeply felt that the right-wing agitation must be countered. This is the reason why the media is full of ethnicity rhetoric, and any multicultural project is seen as a countermeasure at the last minute. But is this not a slight exaggeration of the influence of right-wing populism? A sect of overweight Americans, so the story goes, found out that one billion Chinese people were about to make one jump simultaneously and the earth would be pushed out of its orbit. At the same moment, then, the Americans made a counter-jump, saving the world from its doom. Imagine if Swedish media, politicians, and academics for some time stayed clear from any reference to diversity and anti-racism and, as it were, stopped 'holding the wall' – would we then drown in brownish ethnicity discourse, or would this entire congeries of concepts slowly fade away?

Hannah Arendt, Adolf Hitler and the problem of difference

In the 1970s, equality had central stage in the political left. The worker should have the same rights as other social classes. Then, something happened. What equality was back then, difference is today. We are all different, and the more different, the better and more enriching society. This is one of the central premises of the ideology of diversity. Having been detested through the ages – by Marx and Engels all the way up to Olof Palme – difference has today become all but sacrosanct.

A good example is a 2010 web-ad at Malmö University College. The message – entitled 'Adolf Hitler – the enemy of diversity' – is part of the university college's diversity work, and advertises an open lecture where Hitler's crimes are explained as resistance towards diversity.[458] Difference is being 'celebrated' and difference is 'enriching'. Difference and diversity is good while equality and lack of diversity is bad. But why should all these demarcation lines, be they ethnic, religious, or cultural, bring tolerance? Why would distance and lack of understanding foster enthusiasm, solidarity and sympathy? Are not these emotions, rather than the absence of understanding, associated with their presence; a sense of shared views and being equal?

The principle of difference cannot, Kenan Malik notes, 'provide any standards that oblige us to respect the "difference" of others. At best, it invites our indifference to the fate of the Other.' When the sun shines, we just do not care. 'At worst', Malik continues, 'it licenses us to hate and abuse those who are different. Why, after all, should we not abuse and hate them?'[459]

When the National Socialists started their genocide against European Jewry, the Jews were not portrayed as similar to the Germans, but on the contrary, as an odd and distant breed. It is uncertain whether the Holocaust ever had come under sway if the Berlin propaganda machinery, instead of shouting that the Jews were different from the Germans, had insisted that they were similar.

In case the spectacles of diversity are taken off, the picture is suddenly so strange and yet so familiar: respect requires equality, and lack of respect requires difference. Who do we like less? Those who are not like we are. We feel close to our children and to our partner because they are like we are, and we share life together. You may call it reactionary, but that is the way most of us think. According to Hannah Arendt, the extermination of European Jewry was possible only when they were deprived of their humanity, i.e. when they were made different. The Jews, she claims, did not celebrate their enforced difference. They cursed it.[460] Surely Arendt may be questioned – she was a Republican and was prone to idealise the workers and political commitment. But should not the political implications of equality and difference, at least, be subject to discussion? This is a university, is it not?

From redistribution to recognition

What are the economic consequences when diversity is being promoted so energetically? In her article, 'From Redistribution to Recognition? Dilemmas of Justice in a "Post-Socialist" *Age*,' Nancy Fraser sketches a dark scenario. When group interests replace class interest as a primary basis for political mobilisation, cultural 'dominance supplants exploitation as the fundamental injustice. And cultural recognition displaces socioeconomic redistribution as the remedy for injustice and the goal of political struggle'.[461] Instead of economic redistribution along the lines of the classic leftist paroles of equality, it is about cultural recognition according to diversity's rhetoric of difference.

If, Fraser insists, the central idea of diversity is about an 'intact cultural structure', why, then, should not the rich fight for the right of the poor to remain poor? [462] Behind a veneer of progressivism, the ideology of diversity can be accused of being reactionary and to undermine social change. We used to worry about our own finances. Now we celebrate the poverty of others. You cannot take for granted that any neoliberal who fights on behalf of the cultural and 'ethnic' rights of the poor always means what he or she says.

The last thing the working class needs is recognition of its difference. On the contrary, the only way to remedy the injustice is to put the proletariat out of business as a group.[463] The gap between the cool ideology of diversity and classic leftist demands for reform can hardly be expressed more clearly. What would Friedrich Engels' *The Condition of the Working-class in England in* 1844 have looked like in case he had observed the miners' existence with his eyes full of tenderness[464]? In case multiculturalism had emerged during the 19th century, what would have happened to socialism and the workers' movement?

Presence or ideas?

In her book *The Politics of Presence*, Anne Phillips asks: What should be of prime focus in parliament, at the university and in other types of communities?[465] Should we focus on presence – i.e. the presence of ethnic and other groups? Or should we stress ideas? What, in other words, forms the basis for identification with another human being?

Phillips herself acknowledges that both perspectives are important. We cannot, on the one hand, ignore the ethnic component. We are all to some degree group members. On the other hand, Phillip adds, ideas are important, and must not be pushed aside by the ideology of ethnicity. Sympathy and antipathy must not, as one of the ambitious ideas in modern society, be based on clan belonging – i.e. by our looks, but by the things we say, i.e. by our ideas. Ideas reach beyond clan and tribe, ethnicity *does not*. Ideas give room for other types of kinship than the one written on our skin or in volumes filled with nationalist kitsch.

What about the diversity plans? What do they say? Identity and recognition come via ethnic belonging. The plan at Stockholm University says: How can we counter a sense of alienation and create identity? By making sure that 'the employees mirror the ethnical mix in society, because only then can everybody feel recognized'.[466] The diversity plan at Lund University says: 'It is important that the entire population is being mirrored also in higher education'.[467] 'It is important that Linköping university', their *Equality plan* claims, 'has the competence needed in order to ensure an appropriate activity and', it continues, 'it is of importance that society's diversity is mirrored at the university in order to establish trust and legitimacy'.[468] Research conducted at the institution, the then Director at Malmö University College insists, 'will profit and become more exciting in case we in a fruitful manner manage to make use of the diversity of competences and backgrounds among our (…) employees'. 'We constantly endeavour', he continues, 'to recruit people with a broad range of backgrounds and competences'.[469] 'During recruitment advertising', as stated in the plan at Lund university, 'our ambition about diversity should be clarified'.[470] According to the diversity plan at Uppsala University, it is 'crucial for our quality of future research and education to continue to draw upon a rich exchange of knowledge with a deep respect for students, researchers and teachers with roots in various sociocultural environments'.[471]

Whenever we talk about a diversity of competences, background, and experiences, this shall not be interpreted in their individualist meaning. They are tied to ethnic and other contexts. When the diversity plans in Stockholm and Lund make use of a mirror metaphor, the idea is that identification is made visually. A black person feels 'recognised' in another black person, an Indonesian in another Indonesian, I in my light-skinned neighbour and so on. Identification and a sense of belonging are created via 'presence' – i.e. proximity of other individuals whose bodily qualities resemble my own.

We become mute exhibitionists with our ethnic peculiarities on display. The diversity plans advocate a collectivist form of diversity where the unique qualities of the individual are suppressed; never – precisely – political or scientific views, methods, and independent, perhaps provocative ideas of the individual, student or researcher. It is all about the visual and the collectivist, never about the individual and the abstract. While Swedish higher learning prides itself of its depth and critical thinking, a primitivist, all but Rousseauan idea of community is being cultivated revolving around surface and visual recognition. As surprising as it may seem, the authors behind these antimodernist ideals are seen as progressive. This is a critique from the left.

The university is happy to speak about ethnic diversity, but less prone to talk about the very idea of a university – a variety of *ideas*. Perhaps today's extreme openness for outer, optical and physiological diversity is an indication of an escalating intellectual stagnation? Be tolerant. Let a thousand ethnicities blossom. This is an order.

One reservation. The plan at Göteborg University – named *Policy for Equal Treatment*, is rather silent on the topic of diversity. The plans in the previous discussion, for instance, agreed that the presence of ethnic groups gives identity and success while ideas are of minor importance. What counts is, in other words, not what you do but who you are. At Göteborg University, the tone is different. Having stated that the university must offer excellent opportunities for students from all walks of life, they say this: 'What matters is always what you do, not who you are'.[472] Surprising and beautiful.

International critique

Finally, a few comments on international discussions. A number of these have already been mentioned: the feminist Anne Phillips at the London School of Economics and Political Science, the liberal author and journalist Kenan Malik, the republican and radical Hannah Arendt, and Nancy Fraser – left-wing critic of neoliberalism. In *The Multicultural mistake – What to do in order to live better together in Germany* (*Der Multikulti-Irrtum – Wie wir in Deutschland besser zusammenleben können*), Seyran Ates claims that the entire idea of diversity is a mistake creating enclavisation and antagonism, although its protagonists energetically argue the other way around.[473] Ates also pledges in favour of a European canon drawing on the ideas of the Enlightenment about secularism and pluralism on an individual basis. Slavoj Žižek maintains that multiculturalism is 'hegemonic' and that this is an 'empirical fact'.[474] The intellectual collapse of multiculturalism, claims Perry Anderson, 'does not need to be further underscored: while the Enlightenment, not to mention radical and socialist movements, in anticipation expected any belief in the supranational would eventually vanish, the official and left-liberal opinion now celebrated their swift recovery, as if 'the more religion there was, the better'.[475]

Many more can be added to this international critical discussion. Already in 1995, Christopher Lasch published his *The Revolt of the Elites and the Betrayal of Democracy.* Lasch accuses the elites – 'the speaking classes' – of being more interested in defining agendas and explaining what can be talked about and what not – than in real democracy and dialogue with the people. A Swedish book in the spirit of Lasch is yet to be published.[476] As critics of multiculturalism – and in particular of their own religion – Islam – Hamed Abdel-Samad and Ayaan Hirsi-Ali have both been widely recognised internationally.[477] As yet, no such analysis is available from a Swedish standpoint. In *Culture and Equality – An Egalitarian Critique of Multiculturalism*, the universalist Brian Barry claims that the advocates of multiculturalism make a mistake. Instead of paving the way for equality and freedom, their misconceived agitation leads to authoritarian thinking and to inequality.[478] In *The Politics of Separation: Multiculturalism – Ideology and Reality* (*Adskillelsens politik: multikulturalisme – ideologi og virkelighed,*) Jens Martin Eriksen and Frederik Stjernfelt offer an extensive historical exposé of the critique against multiculturalism.[479] Multiculture does not, they claim, lead to integration but to enclavisation. In the late 1990s, the feminist Susan Moller Okin published *Is Multiculturalism Bad for Women?* where she, among other things insisted that – through the ideology of multiculturalism – women are trapped in patriarchal structures.[480] The British researcher Rumy Hasan recently published *Multiculturalism – Some Inconvenient Truths*, where the author criticised one of multiculturalism's central premises: parallel societies within one state.[481]

This range of academic critique may be supplemented with statements by European leaders outside Sweden. 'The basic idea of multiculti has failed, utterly failed!' Angela Merkel declared in a 2010 speech in Potsdam.[482] Early 2011, 'state supported multiculturalism' was subject to critique by David Cameron: 'Frankly, we need a lot less of the passive tolerance of recent years and much more active, muscular liberalism'.[483] During a TV-discussion only a few days later, Nicolas Sarkozy – the then French President – joined the critique. To the question whether multiculturalism does not work he said: 'My answer is with no doubt yes, it is a failure.'[484] Already in 2005, in a speech at Georgetown University, the former Spanish Prime Minister José María Aznar claimed to oppose 'the idea of multiculturalism. Multiculturalism divides our societies, debilitates our societies, multiculturalism does not produce tolerance, or integration. (…) To accept different laws, depending on the origin of ethnic societies or the religion is a very serious mistake in our society'.[485] This important international discussion has gone unnoticed in Sweden.

While our academics are happy to deconstruct over breakfast, they choose not to question diversity. Why? Are they afraid – of ending up in a centrifuge of associations where anything you say *might* be interpreted as X that may give votes to Y? In the newspaper *Dagens Nyheter* and in the monthly *Axess*, a Professor in the History of Ideas at Lund University, had questioned multiculturalism. In return, he was portrayed as Count Dracula in *Sydsvenskan* – the leading newspaper in southern Sweden – who 'like a coward shies away from the logical implications of his own reasoning'. The only thing that tells the Professor apart from Anders Behring Breivik, the author added, was 'the very aspect of war in their cultural war'.[486] An unfair comparison, to put it mildly. And, by the way, what logical implications? The article illustrates one of the key ideas in this book: anyone who is on the side of multiculturalism stands above logic.

Or is the reason why multiculturalism is not questioned the fear of misunderstandings? The author himself lost an old friend who said I was 'on the barricades of *Sverigedemokraterna*', because I was against multiculturalism. Or – yet again – is the reason simply the pleasure of sharing the opinions of all the others, along with the bliss of never being questioned? What have we gained when all these critics of diversity – Marxists, feminists, republicans and radicals, EU-sceptics, liberals and universalists – are put next to fascists, racists, Nazis and others on the extreme right? Does this make the debate more vigorous? Does it make it less polarised? Does this *decrease* the support for right-wing extreme movements? Our universities ought to be the last refuge of a nuanced political discussion. Why, then, do they not have the stature to oppose outright populism? In Sweden, critics of multiculturalism are a badly treated minority. Does this strengthen respect for dissenting views?

Autonomy or compliance – how did the universities respond?

We must now return to the initial question: How did the universities respond to the task the Social Democratic government had commissioned for them? In order to suggest an answer, the central ideas as expressed in *Diversity at the University* will be compared to the diversity plans at Sweden's eight largest universities.

'Diversity leads to quality,' says the Social Democratic report. The line of reasoning is a political mantra – emotionally powerful but scientifically thin. What do the plans say? Diversity is obvious, self-evident and natural. Diversity leads to quality, and assures quality. In terms of this very central thesis, the diversity plans respond with compliance. No questions asked.

In *Diversity at the University*, an optical definition of diversity is being used. Variation is created by outer qualities, much like you fill an aquarium with decoration fish. How does Swedish academia respond to this attack against intellectual life? With unequivocal enthusiasm, reproducing the conclusions in the report: 'Representation' and 'identification' are made visually according to your pigmentation. A European cannot recognise himself in his chess-playing friend from Tunisia. The plans reproduce social democratic ethno-pessimism. The modern project is creaking at the edges.

Diversity, announces *Diversity at the University*, is intimately linked to internationalisation and creates bridges between cultures. The truth appears to be the opposite: diversity tears down bridges and erects walls between human beings and between groups. None of Sweden's eight largest universities picks up the theme.

Diversity is anti-racism, insists the report. Multiculturalism rests on a progressive, tolerant, and egalitarian foundation where tensions are overcome and we make friends. A scientific discussion should also allow for the opposite point of view, where diversity and racism are two branches of early 19th century political romanticism. The university, however, fails its intellectual mission (the only 'mission' a university has), deteriorating into a mindless trumpet for Social Democratic pseudo-radicalism.

Diversity at the University takes on all ideas that seem sympathetic, even if they from an analytical point of view are irreconcilable. Diversity is mixed up with the welfare state and with the autonomous individual. But why so silent about the concept of solidarity, the virtue *not* paying attention to borders – ethnic, class-based, and otherwise? Whatever happens to diversity as a social form of organisation in case the ethnic group has swinging-doors? If the woman is allowed to be a master of her own life? In the diversity plans these urgent questions are all but absent. According to *Diversity at the University*, the alphabet starts and ends with cultural recognition. Multiculturalism, left-wing critics maintain, puts a blind eye to the aspect of class and economic recognition, which makes it fit like a glove on the hand of the neoliberal. Where is the criticism? The leftist critique draws our attention to various forms of connection between diversity and neoliberalism. Economically fragile groups attack one another while the caravan of Brussels carries on. From this perspective, the ideology of diversity stands in stark opposition to the interests of the poor. No comment.

Finally: In their diversity work, the report suggested, the universities and university colleges should receive 2.5 billion Swedish kronor over five years. Thereafter, economic supply should 'vary according to degree of success in diversity work'.[487] At this particular time, the Swedish university was in a state of underfinanced brisk expansion. Perhaps this was seen as a financial opportunity not to be missed during turbulent times, and all ideological considerations were subsequently put aside. Today we know what happened. It was a suggestion, not a promise. The Social Democratic government abandoned its own report. The sum was modified to 40 million over three years; i.e. 120 million and slightly below five per cent of what had previously been proposed.[488] From a Social Democratic perspective, this was an achievement politically as well as financially. Virtually for free, diversity had become a founding pillar in

Swedish higher education. The scenario is a good case of mismanagement of state power: ideological pressure throughout the entire system, politicisation of intellectual life, lofty financial declarations that all come to naught, demands on academics to *ignore* fundamental issues (such as the division between ethnicity and class), and so on. Still, all remains silent in the land of Sweden – which further strengthens my conviction that Swedish academia lacks independence.

A way out?

Multiculturalism has failed concerning the independence of the university, regarding ideological debate and critical thinking. It has undermined autonomy among researchers and lecturers. It has infiltrated panels, projects, institutes, faculties, offices, courses, and curricula. Last but not least it has let the students down. Instead of showing them how to think, it has told them what to think. This is the failure of multiculturalism.

Perhaps there is a way out. In case the international criticism finally reaches Sweden, we just might, as proposed by Robert Putnam, leave the crooked suspicion of ethnicity towards a more inclusive sense of 'us' and transgressing solidarity. Three factors may decide whether this scenario will work out or not.

The first aspect has to do with the university's intellectual autonomy. Ideological whips filled with moralism shall not dictate a site of higher learning and values deemed 'good'. Goodness is a notoriously unreliable argument – fascists, too, believe they do good things. If you wish to oppose those who advocate racism, you must not advocate anti-racism. You should do nothing at all. Academia receives a steady and rising number of tasks 'commissioned' by politicians. The university's only 'task', however, is to protect its intellectual independence. This task is on the shoulders of each and every academic. Hired consultants, 'experts' and therapists should be regarded with suspicion unless proven otherwise. In particular, academia must be on guard against bureaucratic proposals. *Invariably*, they contain one ideology or another. The only way 'profile areas' or 'cultures' may emerge at a university is when it is the result of research. The university shall be quiet, and the researchers shall speak, not the other way around.

When advocates of diversity attack the university for lacking in visions, they assume that satisfaction and engagement comes from the university, *and not* from independent research. Religious people, for the same reason, believe a society resting on the free choice of the individual is 'cold' and 'without meaning'. The university is constantly threatened by myths. When a university offers 'support', it often means: mental correction. 'Information' is manipulation, 'dialogue' means to convince, 'gain appreciation' is *fait accompli*. Orwellian New Speak constantly jeopardises intellectual independence.

The second aspect is about the classic ideal of education. Multiculturalism is hostile towards knowledge and anti-intellectual. At this point, the classic ideal of education offers a corrective. According to this ideal, nothing is ever self-evident or the object of ostensibly neutral information. Nothing is seen as 'above and beyond' discussion.

Everything has to be subject to open discussion. The classic ideal of education is not about who is right, but about the hope that we will be enlightened by discussions and evidence. It is about education but also about knowledge; not about certainty based on emotions, but about scepticism resting on science. Viewpoints are accepted without being subject to psychological manipulation. This ideal is not exposed to political proposals and ideologies. Unless something is properly defined, it can neither be defended nor criticised. This distinguishes academia from religion.

According to the classic ideal of education, any view must be internally consistent. Contradictory views cannot be combined. This ideal evades political clichés and jargon. The very idea is to find the most subtle shades and nuances in all questions imaginable. You cannot separate the world into black and white – or friends and enemies. The classic ideal of education lacks prestige. All knowledge is therefore a good thing. All ideas mean that knowledge is growing, whether one particular thought is strengthened or weakened. This is scientific collectivism and modernity in fusion. According to the classical ideal of education, we do not, as intellectual beings, recognise ourselves in what we see, but in what we hear. The basis for kinship and animosity is not the colour of the skin, but ideas. This ideal does not suggest mute exhibitionists, but dazzling conversations between peers and equals; not a 'colourful mosaic' of cultural differences but, in the words of Martin Luther King, a colour blind society focusing on our intellectual life.

The third aspect has to do with restoring the independent student. When the student is seen primarily as an exponent for his/her culture, this has a number of consequences. The autonomy is threatened because he/she constantly must take this background into account. The student is expected to surrender to the 'community leader' and 'spokesperson' – who just might have other political views. The student is taken 'hostage by his/her cultural, ethnic group' and is invited into an ever-present grab-and-scramble meal about whose culture has suffered the most, and whose acts of revenge are most righteous. In turn, knowledge is being politicised, relativized, and, as a science, it ceases to exist.[489] The students, instead of being offered a variety and 'diversity' of knowledge, are transformed into pre-programmed bureaucrats. We make the students angry and fragile, when we ought to make them strong and happy. Students should not be noted for their suffering but for their accomplishments. The student is locked into his/her culture, which in particular has serious repercussions for women. Common ideas are wiped aside for the benefit of 'shared roots' and herd mentality – a drunken wish for the exploiters and upper classes. I do not criticise diversity from a conservative point of view. I criticise diversity because it is conservative.

A Trojan horse

This is a case study. The discussion has been about how the university is affected by diversity, but my purpose goes beyond this. How does diversity affect society at large? The overriding impression is that diversity is not what we think. The societal consequences are, therefore, also not what we hope they would be.

We believe it is emancipating but it turns individuals into prisoners of their roots. We believe it is modern, while, in fact, it leads to the return of religion. We think it creates debate when it leads to censorship. We believe it is political when it actually puts its jackboot on all things political. The ethnic representative may freely ignore political qualifications and the *only* demarcation lines deemed irrelevant are political ones. The roots of diversity, it is widely held, go back to the political philosophy of the left, and yet it speaks very little about class but very much about culture. What would Marx have said? We believe it is critical against power when, in fact, power is allowed to separate and antagonise underprivileged groups – i.e. divide and rule. We would disagree if someone said it is conservative, but if you talk about nothing but background and roots you are conservative. We believe is fosters minorities as such, but the only minorities supported are those who oppose the modern world, while those who wish to move towards it are left alone. We see diversity as anti-populism but the image of the elevated ethnic spokesperson has the flavour of a right-wing populist leader cult. Authentic and 'real life' depictions of ethnic groups on TV are unflinchingly supported, while, in fact, they are a death kiss to artistic freedom. We believe diversity fosters equal opportunities, but it is bad for women. We think it gives us a voice, but we are transformed into mute exhibitionists. We believe its perspective is from underneath, but diversity is an upper-class mark, a slap in the face of unrefined workers. Diversity, we maintain, is a weapon against the bourgeoisie, but according to diversity you must act 'modestly' and see to your 'reputation'. A religion that invokes the death penalty if you criticise the nuclear family is defended by politicians who speak about the death of the nuclear family. We oppose racial concepts and build our entire structure on racial concepts. We mistake etiquette for ideology: Help yourself, first, please, with the outer knives and forks. Pity first, please, distant minority groups. We oppose 'the past', but still seek identification with the herd instincts of wild animals. We are fascinated by the 'Others' even when they utter trivialities and know it. We say we oppose ethnic tensions, but in fact we fabricate ethnic tensions to give fuel to our social pessimism and arguments for our projects. We love exotic customs, but only the pleasant ones. We are 'left' and yet we demolish the society created by Social Democracy. We celebrate diversity, in which the poor have the right to remain poor. The culture of others is deep, authentic, and does not withstand inner friction – all classic political romanticism with more than a scent of the 1930s. We are anti-racists and defend difference, which enabled the genocide of European Jewry. We believe diversity is left, but it is right. Diversity is an attack against modernity. The Western world has dragged a Trojan horse into it's midst.

Notes

1. Wild, wild, West. Movie, 1999.
2. Does TV Capture the Diversity of America Yet?, internet source.
3. BBC – Everyone has a story. The BBC's Diversity Strategy 2011-15, internet source.
4. French Diversity Charter, internet source.
5. Salto stands for Support, Advanced Learning and Training Opportunities within the European YOUTH programme.
6. A guide to European diversity, internet source.
7. French Diversity Charter, internet source.
8. BBC – Everyone has a story. The BBC's Diversity Strategy 2011-15, internet source.
9. Survey on cultural diversity, internet source.
10. Umgang mit Migrantinnen und Migranten – Multikulturalismus in Kanada – Modell für Deutschland?, internet source.
11. EDA – European Diversity Awards, internet source.
12. BBC – Everyone has a story. The BBC's Diversity Strategy 2011-15, internet source.
13. A guide to European diversity, internet source.
14. Teachers Initial Training in Cultural Diversity in Spain: Attitudes and Pedagogical Strategies, internet source.
15. A guide to European diversity, internet source.
16. Ibid.
17. BBC – Everyone has a story. The BBC's Diversity Strategy 2011-15, internet source.
18. Diversity charters across the EU, internet source.
19. A guide to European diversity, internet source.
20. Canadian Multiculturalism: An Inclusive Citizenship, internet source.
21. BBC – Everyone has a story. The BBC's Diversity Strategy 2011-15, internet source.
22. Fremde Kulturen im europäischen Fernsehen, internet source.
23. Approach to cultural diversity in Italy, internet source.
24. A guide to European diversity, internet source.
25. BBC – Everyone has a story. The BBC's Diversity Strategy 2011-15, internet source.
26. Mission – Organisation for Friendship in Diversity (OFD, Malta), internet source.
27. The Challenge of French Diversity, internet source.
28. For Diversity. Against Discrimination. this year's EU award-winning articles, internet source.
29. French Diversity Charter, internet source.
30. Spain implements a practical approach to managing diversity! – Council of Europe, internet source.
31. BBC – Everyone has a story. The BBC's Diversity Strategy 2011-15, internet source.
32. Italy Gives Cultural Diversity a Lukewarm Embrace, internet source.
33. For an extensive survey about the concept of populism,
See Adamson, 2009.
34. Myndigheters mångfaldsarbete Delrapport 1, 2007, p. 31, internet source.
35. Rasismens olika ansikten – Skolans värdegrund, p. 1; Mångfald och likvärdighet – Skolans värdegrund, internet sources.

36 Etnisk och kulturell mångfald, p. 1, internet source.
37 Innovation genom mångfald när nya svenska möter landsbygden,
38 Mångfald, Polismyndigheten i Stockholms län, p. 1, internet source.
39 Heliga danser för mångfald, rättvisa och hållbarhet (32), p. 1, internet source.
40 Regleringsbrev för Budgetåret 2008 avseende Statens Haverikommission, p. 1, internet source.
41 Integration och mångfald, p. 1, internet source. Since 2011, the heading has changed. Then, it was labelled Integration och mångfald. At the time of writing (2012-01-19) the title is Integration. The government's internal link to the page is still called Integration och mångfald.
42 Vänsterpartiet mångfald as Google search, internet source.
43 MP: Vi har en härlig mångfald, p. 1, internet source.
44 Mångfald – Ger mervärde och affärsnytta, p. 1, internet source.
45 Mångfald berikar, p. 1, internet source.
46 Förbundet Liberal Mångfald – Liberal Mångfald, p. 1, internet source.
47 Mångfald – framgångsfaktor för hållbar tillväxt, p. 1, internet source.
48 Integration och mångfald, p. 1, internet source.
49 Ansvarsfull invandringspolitik, p. 1, internet source.
50 Lundquist, 2012, p. 44. See also Flyvbjerg, 2006.
51 Wood, 2003.
52 Phillips, 2006.
53 Scruton, 2002.
54 Caldwell, 2010.
55 Steyn, 2006.
56 Krönika: Den radikala kampmetoden är den enda rätta!, internet source
57 Nordfront – Det fria Nordens röst, internet source.
58 Nationaldemokraterna – Våra viktigaste frågor, internet source.
59 Hasan, 2010.
60 Malik, 2010.
61 Phillips, 2010.
62 Eriksen and Stjernfelt, 2008, p. 219.
63 Ibid., p. 14.
64 Barry, 2001.
65 Bawer, 2006.
66 See for instance Kowalsky & Schroeder, 1994; Kowalsky, 1992.
67 Cohen, 2007. Bech Dyrberg, 2008, p. 4.
68 Demirbag-Sten & Bauhn, 2010.
69 Falsafi, 2004.
70 Cwejman, 2012.
71 Alvesson, 2006; Alvesson and Svengsson, 2012.
72 Bortom Multikulti, internet source.
73 Multiculturalism is communism, internet source; Scruton, 2010, p. 160.
74 Bobbio, 1995.
75 Bernard Crick, p. 1, internet source.
76 Mångfald i högskolan, p. 3
77 Oktober 21, Docent Anders Persson was appointed Secretary and Lars Eriksson was appointed as Project leader, Nov 9, 1999, Prof. Björn Fryklund, Lektor Elisabeth Gerle, Rektor Tom Hagman, Adjunkt Mohsen Hakim, Diversity Manager Aleksandra Kovacevic, Avdelningsdirektör Irja Persson Utterhall, Kammarrättsnotarie Björn Andersson, Rektor Marianne Persson samt Stud. Kristian Populin were appointed as experts. March 29, Populin was replaced by Stud. Kathrin Österlund. Other participants were Stud. Biljana Matevska, and Stud. Shervin Hedayat. Executive Officer Eivor Terneacted as the committée administrator of the investigation.See Mångfald i högskolan, p. 4.

78 Mångfald i högskolan reflektioner och förslag om social och etnisk mångfald i högskolan (SOU 2000:47) (Below in abbreviation – Mångfald i högskolan). Mångfald i högskolan (Diversity at the university) has gone rather unnoticed in the debate. As one exception, an author in *Universitetsläraren* (7/2013), defended the report's ambition to maintain quality at the university. (Thormark, p. 16)
79 Mångfald i högskolan, p.15.
80 Utvärdering av arbetet med breddad rekrytering till universitet och högskolor, p. 9, internet source.
81 Roth, 1996, p. 12.
82 Among critics, this definition sometimes goes under the name of boutique multiculturalism.
83 Mångfald i högskolan, p. 9.
84 Ibid.
85 Ibid.
86 Ibid., p.15.
87 Ibid., p. 23.
88 Ibid., p. 17.
89 Löfgren & Wadstein, 1999, p. 16.
90 Mångfald i högskolan, p. 13.
91 Ibid.
92 Ibid.
93 Ibid., p. 16f.
94 Orwell, p. 121.
95 Mångfald i högskolan, p. 4.
96 Ibid., p. 110.
97 Ibid., p. 57.
98 Ibid., p. 112.
99 Ibid., p. 113.
100 Ibid., p. 127.
101 Ibid.
102 Ibid.
103 Ibid., p. 15.
104 Ibid., p. 127.
105 Ibid., p. 14, p. 128.
106 Ibid., p. 107.
107 Ibid., p. 102.
108 Ibid., p. 116.
109 Ibid., p. 106.
110 Ibid., p. 87.
111 Koestler, 1954, p. 77.
112 Persson, 2011, interview.
113 Mångfald i högskolan, p. 107.
114 Hasan, 2010.
115 Mångfald i högskolan, p. 1.
116 Ibid., p. 14.
117 Ibid., p. 102.
118 Golsan, 1998, p. 54.
119 Putnam, 2007.
120 Ibid., p. 144.
121 Ibid., p. 140. See also Simonton, 1999.
122 See for instance Webber & Donahue, 2001; O'Reilly et al., 1997; Williams & O'Reilly, 1998; Page, 2007.
123 Putnam, p. 140.
124 Ibid., s 141f; Stouffer, 1949.
125 Blumer, 1958; Blalock, 1967; Giles & Evans, 1986; Quillian, 1995 och 1996; Brewer & Brown, 1998; Taylor, 1998; Bobo, 1999; Bobo and Tuan, 2006.
126 Jackson et at, 1991; Cohen & Bailey, 1997; Keller, 2001; Webber & Donahue, 2001.
127 Newton & Delhey, 2005; Andersson & Paskeviciute, 2006; Hooghe et al, 2006.
128 Poterba, 1997; Alesina et al., 1999; Alesina & La Farrara, 2000 och 2002; Costa & Kahn, 2003; Vigdor, 2004; Glaeser & Alesina, 2004; Leigh, 2006; Jordahl & Gustavsson, 2006; Soroka et al., 2007; Pennant, 2005.
129 Charles & Kline, 2002; Putnam, 142-3.
130 Putnam, p. 147.
131 Alvesson, 2006, p. 150.
132 Putnam, p. 149.
133 See for instance Tönnies, 1935, and Durkheim, 2006.
134 Putnam, p. 149-50.
135 Alba och Nee, 2003, p. 32.
136 Putnam, p. 159.
137 Ibid., p. 164.
138 Putnam, p. 163-4.
139 Bauman, 2001.
140 Putnam, p. 165.

141 I have the potential of Bringing People Together.
142 See for instance Webber & Donahue, 2001; O'Reilly et al., 1997; Williams & O'Reilly, 1998. Page, 2007; Putnam, p. 140.
143 Sichrowsky, 2002, interview.
144 For an extensive discussion around this general question, see Finkelstein, 2000.
145 Mångfald i högskolan, p. 106 and p. 87.
146 Lundquist, 2012, p. 134.
147 Ibid., p. 87.
148 Mångfald i högskolan, p. 1.
149 Kommittédirektiv – Social och etnisk mångfald i högskolan, 1999.
150 Ibid., p. 127.
151 Persson, 2011, interview.
152 Ibid.
153 Mångfald i högskolan, p. 1.
154 Persson, 2011, interview.
155 Persson, 2001, p. 1-2, internet source.
156 Anderson, 2009, p. 527f.
157 Mångfald i högskolan, p. 106.
158 Ibid., p. 14.
159 Kommittédirektiv – Social och etnisk mångfald i högskolan, 1999, p. 1.
160 Mångfald i högskolan, p. 1.
161 Ibid., p. 70.
162 Ibid.
163 Ibid., p. 126.
164 Ibid., p. 103.
165 Ibid., p. 11.
166 Ibid., p. 56; p. 104.
167 Ibid., p. 8.
168 Ibid., p. 61.
169 Ibid. See also Andersson, 1999.
170 Mångfald i högskolan, p. 15.
171 Ibid., p. 11.
172 Ibid., p. 15.
173 Ibid., p. 102.
174 Ibid., p. 63.
175 Ibid.
176 Canovan, 1992, p. 63–98.
177 Mångfald i högskolan, p. 109.
178 Webster, 1997, p. 9.
179 Black & Lakhani, 1997, p. 13–33.
180 Stasiulis, 1997, p. 1, internet source.
181 Asante, 1991–92, p. 29.
182 Mångfald i högskolan, p. 108.
183 Ibid., p. 109.
184 Ibid., p. 14.
185 Ibid., p. 63.
186 Webster, p. 46.
187 Banner-Haley, p. 663–665.
188 Laqueur, 2011, p. 257.
189 Hasan, 2010, p. 268.
190 Mångfald i högskolan, p. 1.
191 The BBC illustrates another problem with ethnic representation as an idea. Portrayal of life in modern Britain states the webpage, should be authentic. The percentage of minority groups in shows such as *East Enders* must, hence, properly reflect the percentage of minority groups in reality. Unless it does, it is no longer authentic. But wait a second. Who, historically speaking, kept insisting that art must always be authentic? Who said that any kind of deviation from 'reality' was improper? Who shrugged in the face of artistic licence? The moralists and the reactionaries. *Entartete Kunst* – the 1937 Nazi exhibition in Berlin of 'degenerate art' – is a good case in point. The entire jargon around authentic depictions and authentic existence is saturated with political romanticism. It also, at least by implication, threatens one of the key ideas of culture – namely our capacity for *imagination*, for instance when our impression of a great play is not ruined by a minimalist theatre scenography, or when Daniel Day Lewis may portray Abraham Lincoln, although Lewis is actually 2 inches shorter. In order to buttress its theories, multiculturalism cannot, as it seems, do without all sorts of bourgeois and deeply conservative paraphernalia. (See BBC – Everyone has a story. The BBC's Diversity Strategy 2011-15.)

192 Orwell, Notes on Nationalism, internet source.
193 See also Adamson, Masochist Nationalism – Multicultural Self-hatred and the Enchantment with the Exotic, unpublished manuscript.
194 Mona Sahlin: Sverigedemokraternas bästa vän!, p. 1, internet source.
195 Kowalsky, 1992, p. 64.
196 Mer monstruöst och hemskt kan det kulturella självförnekandet knappast vara.
197 Orwell, Notes on Nationalism, internet source.
198 For an interesting but slightly rhetorical discussion about the excessive self-criticism in the West, see Bruckner, 2010. For an extensive critique of this view from a Swedish horizon, see Lundberg, 2013.
199 Mångfald i högskolan, p. 12.
200 Ibid., p. 59.
201 Eriksson och Jonsson, 1993, p. 118.
202 Mångfald i högskolan, p. 59. See also Reuterberg, 1999.
203 Mångfald i högskolan, p. 4.
204 Ibid., p. 102.
205 Ibid., p. 126.
206 Ibid., p. 128.
207 Ibid.
208 Ibid., p. 10.
209 Ibid., p. 15.
210 Crick, 1984, p. 13; Serge, 1984.
211 Mångfaldskonsult, och Mångfaldskonsulent. A Google search gives above 2,000 hits on the former and above 1,000 on the latter.
212 Mångfald i högskolan, p. 4.
213 Alvesson, 2006, p. 149.
214 Žižek, 1997, p. 46.
215 Ibid., p. 44.
216 Anderson, 2009, p. 537.
217 Ibid., p. 537f.
218 Barry, 2001, p. 11.
219 Ibid., p. 534.
220 Žižek, 2000, p. 37f.
221 French National Front's black and Arab supporters, internet source.
222 Bech Dyrberg, 2008, p. 7.
223 Aktiva åtgärder för att främja etnisk mångfald i arbetslivet, 1999, p. 16. Cited in Mångfald i högskolan, p. 105.
224 Bourdieu, 2000, p. 51.
225 Ibid., p. 131, 134.
226 Friedman, 2002, p. 38.
227 See for instance Hasan, 2008, p. 225.
228 Gerle, 1999, p. 166.
229 Hylland Eriksen, 1999, p. 63.
230 Friedman, 2009, p. 5.
231 Eriksen & Stjernfelt, 2008, p. 300.
232 Žižek, 2000, p. 37f.
233 Engels, 1968.
234 Orwell 2001, p. 156.
235 Ibid., p. 106.
236 Hummer & Pelinka, 2002, p. 287.
237 Bech & Necef, 2013, p. 44.
238 Hayek, *Individualism and Economic Order*, in particular Ch. XII.
239 Hayek, *Law, Legislation and Liberty*, 3 Volumes.
240 Hayek, *Law, legislation and Liberty*, Vol. 2, p. 111 f.
241 Sörensen, 2014, p. 26.
242 Friedman, 2002, p. 42.
243 Mångfald i högskolan, p. 52.
244 Ibid., p. 53.
245 Ibid., p. 61.
246 Ibid., p. 72.
247 Ibid., p. 50.
248 Ibid., p. 52.
249 Betz, 2000, p. 268.
250 Riedlsperger, 1996, p. 359.
251 Kowalsky, 1992, p. 32.
252 Riedsperger, 1996, p. 360.
253 Westman, 2005, intervju.
254 Prasad & Prasad, cited in Alvesson, 2006, p. 151.
255 Žižek, 1999, p. 219.
256 Carlbom, 2003, p. 46.
257 Anderson, 2009, p. 533.
258 Pluralism i mångfald, internet source.
259 Taggart, 2000, p. 21.
260 Adamson, 2014.
261 Persson, 2001, p. 2, internet source.
262 Mångfald i högskolan, p. 51.

263 Žižek, 1997, p. 47.

264 From afar, the discourse of diversity illustrates a broader tendency in academic life – one dominated by pessimism and moralism. An illustrative parallel can be found in psychology and in a quite influential branch within research on sexual abuse – so-called repressed memories. While research on diversity fabricates dark visions about the situation of immigrants in Sweden, the theory of repressed memories invents dark visions about the childhood of the client. In the eyes of psychotherapists working on repressed memories, the clients capacity to remember sexual abuse has something deep and majestic about it. The diversity advocate, on her part, is caught by the grandiose in the life story of immigrants, asserting these stories to the best of her capacity. In order to retain his importance and our fascination for him, confirm our theories, and keep his monthly allowances, the immigrant tells us what we expect him to say. A patient going through the treatment of repressed memories – Sture Bergvall is a good case in point - tells us what we expect him to say in order to confirm our theories, our research and our reputation, and retain his own stature in the scheme. In *The Myth of Repressed Memory*, Lynn, we are told, goes deeper and deeper into this kind of therapy: "Let the gateway open", he encouraged the women. "Don't be afraid." Lynn was afraid. (…) She had always believed that her mother and father had loved and protected her – but why hadn't they saved her from her uncle? Could her therapist be right? Could it be that the people she loved most in the world /…/ had abused her? (Loftus and Ketcham, 1994, p. 11) The danger is constituted by your family, and the way out is to follow the advice of the therapist. When the ideology of diversity – perhaps best illustrated by the term xenophobia – tells us embrace the stranger, this comes at a cost of a weakened proximity to family and friends. Both in terms of utopia and in the dramatic set-up, the scenarios show similarities. It is not about them but about us and our need for entertainment and excitement, and our interest to portray ourselves as important and as morally righteous. The ordinary is not exciting and never was. To the therapist as well as to the multicultural theoretician, it all boils down to one and the same unscientific method: Our right to create the background and history of the Other. We justify our exploitation of them by siding with them, and their plight is in our interest, and the critic, standing in front of this imposing edifice of self-justifications, wavers not only once.

265 Mångfald i högskolan, p. 51.

266 For an overview of these interrelations, see Berlin, in Hardy & Hausheer, 1998. See also Adamson, 2014.

267 Eriksen & Stjernfelt, 2008, p. 132.

268 Mångfald i högskolan, p. 5.

269 Ibid.

270 Adamson, 2002.

271 Lundquist, 2012, p. 163.

272 Eriksson & Jonsson, 1993, p. 118.

273 Mångfald i högskolan, p. 9.

274 Ibid., p. 116.

275 Ibid., p. 75.

276 Ibid., p. 64.

277 Ibid., p. 102.

278 Ibid., p. 104.

279 Ibid., p. 11.

280 Ibid., p. 52.

281 Haider, 1997.

282 Mångfald i högskolan, p. 10.

283 Ibid., p. 134.
284 Ibid.
285 Ibid., p. 13.
286 Ibid., p. 9.
287 Ibid., p. 55.
288 Appiah, 1995, p. 151.
289 Mångfald i högskolan, p. 47.
290 Ibid., p. 56.
291 Ibid., p. 55. See also Roth, 1996, p. 12.
292 Mångfald i högskolan, p. 49.
293 Ibid., p. 11.
294 Eriksen & Stjernfelt, 2008, p. 320.
295 Ates, 2007.
296 Bauhn & Demirbag-Sten, 2010, p. 86.
297 Hasan, 2010, p. 75.
298 Ibid., p. 258. For an extensive discussion on violence against women in ethnic minority groups, see Danneskiold-Samsøe; Mørck & Wagner Sørensen, 2011.
299 Mångfald i högskolan, p. 11.
300 Ibid., p. 3.
301 Rosengård ska krydda Sverige; Xenofilia.se, internet source.
302 Orwell, 2001, p. 106.
303 Jämställdhets- och mångfaldspolicy 2009–2011, p. 5, internet source.
304 Friedman, 2007, p. 437.
305 A colour- and difference blind approach, writes Rumy Hasan, is the safest way to overcome discrimination, and ought to be closely related to John Rawls veil of ignorance, i.e. a theoretical social model in which you do not know you own role in it, and hence contributes to a society characterised by justice. (Hasan, 2010,p. 235; Rawls, 1971, p. 136f). The comment strengthens the picture of multiculturalism as an anti-liberal project.
306 Mångfald i högskolan, p. 52.
307 Ibid.
308 Ibid.
309 Ibid., p. 48.
310 Ibid.
311 Ibid., p. 55.
312 Persson, 2001, p. 2, internet source.
313 Barry, 2001, p. 11.
314 Eriksen & Stjernfelt, 2008, p. 357.
315 Alvesson, 2006, p. 150.
316 Ibid., p. 152.
317 Lundquist, 2012, p. 14.
318 Mångfald i högskolan, p. 15, 127.
319 Universitet & högskolor – Högskoleverkets årsrapport 2011, p. 95, internet source. All of these plans are not called diversity plans, but the concept has been used throughout for the sake of simplicity.
320 Mångfaldsplan för anställda vid Stockholms universitet 2007–2011, p. 2, internet source.
321 Ibid.
322 Ibid.
323 Ibid., p. 3.
324 Ibid., p. 2.
325 Ibid.
326 Ibid.
327 Ibid.
328 Mångfaldsplan 2007–2009 rörande etnisk och social tillhörighet samt religion eller annan trosuppfattning med åtgärdsprogram för 2009, p. 7, internet source.
329 Ibid., p. 6.
330 Ibid.
331 Ibid.
332 Ibid.
333 Ibid.
334 Ibid., p. 10.
335 Ibid., p. 9.
336 Ibid., p. 8.
337 Ibid.
338 Ibid.
339 Ibid.
340 Ibid., p. 9.
341 Mångfaldsplan 2009 för anställda vid Lunds Universitet, p. 3, internet source.
342 Ibid.
343 Ibid.
344 Ibid.
345 Ibid.

346 Ibid.
347 Ibid.
348 Mångfald, Lunds Universitet, p. 1, internet source.
349 Ett inkluderande universitet, p. 7, internet source.
350 Ibid., p. 6.
351 Ibid., p. 13.
352 Ibid., p. 4.
353 Ibid., p. 9.
354 Ibid.
355 Ibid., p. 10.
356 Ibid.
357 Ibid.
358 Ibid., p. 11.
359 Ibid., p. 6.
360 Ibid., p. 14.
361 Jämlikhetsplan för Linnéuniversitetet 2011, internet source. An ambitious diversity plan was made in 2003, going through a major revision in 2006. See Mångfaldspolicy för Växjö Universitet 2003, internet source.
362 Jämlikhetsplan för Linnéuniversitetet 2011, p. 3, internet source.
363 Ibid., p. 4.
364 Ibid.
365 Ibid., p. 5.
366 Ibid., p. 8.
367 Ibid., p. 9.
368 Ibid.
369 Jämställdhets- och mångfaldspolicy 2009–2011, p. 6, internet source.
370 Ibid., p. 5.
371 Ibid.
372 Ibid., p. 6.
373 Ibid.
374 Ibid., p. 9.
375 Linköpings Universitets arbete med social och etnisk mångfald, 2003, internet source.
376 Strategi och handlingsplan för lika villkor 2012, p. 3 , internet source.
377 Ibid., p. 1.
378 Ibid., p. 3.
379 Ibid.
380 Ibid.
381 Ibid., p. 9.
382 Ibid.
383 Ibid.
384 Ibid.
385 Ibid.
386 Strategi och handlingsplan för lika villkor 2012, p. 9f, internet source.
387 Ibid., p. 5.
388 Likabehandlingspolicy 2007–2010, p. 3, internet source.
389 Ibid., p. 2.
390 Ibid.
391 Ibid., p. 3.
392 Ibid.
393 Mångfaldsplan för anställda vid Stockholms universitet 2007–2011, p. 3, internet source.
394 Etnicitet, mångfald och integration, 7.5 hp; Masterprogram i intersektionalitetsstudier, 120hp, internet sources.
395 Mångfaldsplan 2007–2009 rörande etnisk och social tillhörighet samt religion eller annan trosuppfattning med åtgärdsprogram för 2009, p. 8, internet source.
396 Ibid., p. 10.
397 Ibid., p. 7.
398 Kandidatprogram i Equality and Diversity Management 180.0 hp, p. 1, internet source.
399 Mångfaldsplan 2009 för anställda vid Lunds Universitet, p. 2, internet source.
400 Socionomprogrammet – Inriktning individ, familj och samhälle, p. 1; Socionomprogrammet – Inriktning funktionshinder och åldrande, p. 1; Socionomprogrammet – Inriktning verksamhetsutveckling, p. 1, internet sources.
401 Perspektivområden, p. 1, internet source.
402 Carlbom, 2003, p. 56.
403 Jämlikhetsplan för Linnéuniversitetet 2011, p. 5, internet source.
404 See for instance Mannheim, 1936.
405 Mångfaldsplan 2009 för anställda

vid Lunds Universitet, p. 3, internet source.

406 Jämställdhets- och mångfalds-policy 2009–2011, p. 3, internet source.

407 Ibid., p. 7.

408 Kandidatprogram i Equality and Diversity Management 180.0 hp, p. 1, internet source.

409 Mångfaldsplan 2007–2009 rörande etnisk och social tillhörighet samt religion eller annan trosuppfattning med åtgärdsprogram för 2009, p. 6, internet source.

410 Jämställdhets- och mångfalds-policy 2009–2011, p. 5, internet source.

411 Mångfaldsplan 2009 för anställda vid Lunds Universitet, p. 2, internet source.

412 Jämställdhets- och mångfalds-policy 2009–2011, p. 3, internet source.

413 Likabehandlingspolicy 2007–2010, p. 2; Mångfaldsplan för anställda vid Stockholms universitet 2007–2011, p. 1, internet sources.

414 Mångfaldsplan 2009 för anställda vid Lunds Universitet, p. 3, internet source.

415 Högskolor och universitet i Sverige, p. 1, internet source.

416 Ambassadörer arbetar för mångfald, s. 1, internet source.

417 Mångfaldsplan 2007–2009 rörande etnisk och social tillhörighet samt religion eller annan trosuppfattning med åtgärdsprogram för 2009, p. 6, internet source.

418 Jämställdhets- och mångfalds-policy 2009–2011, p. 13, internet source.

419 Mångfaldsplan för anställda vid Stockholms universitet 2007–2011, s. 2, internet source.

420 Mångfaldsplan 2009 för anställda vid Lunds Universitet, p. 2, internet source.

421 Lundquist, 2012, p. 29.

422 Ibid., p. 80.

423 Friedman, 2007, p. 452.

424 Sex personer gripna i Kina efter rykten om statskupp, p1, internet source.

425 Mångfaldsplan 2007–2009 rörande etnisk och social tillhörighet samt religion eller annan trosuppfattning med åtgärdsprogram för 2009, p. 4, internet source.

426 Ibid., p. 9.

427 Mångfaldsplan 2009 för anställda vid Lunds Universitet, p. 1, internet source.

428 Mångfald, p. 1, Lunds Universitet, internet source.

429 Mångfaldsplan för anställda vid Stockholms universitet 2007–2011, p. 1, internet source.

430 Strategi och handlingsplan för lika villkor 2012, p. 9, internet source.

431 En resa in i framtiden, p. 16, internet source.

432 Mångfaldsplan 2009 för anställda vid Lunds Universitet, p. 1, internet source.

433 Församlingsinstruktion för Stora Tuna och Torsångs församlingar – Svenska kyrkan i Borlänge, p. 7; Karlskoga Folkhögskola, p. 1, internet sources.

434 Mångfaldsplan för anställda vid Stockholms universitet 2007–2011, p. 1, internet source.

435 Mångfald, Lunds Universitet, p.1, internet source.

436 Lasch, 1995, p. 67.

437 Mångfald, Lunds Universitet, p.1, internet source.

438 Strategi och handlingsplan för lika villkor 2012, p. 9, internet source.

439 Mångfaldsplan för anställda vid Stockholms universitet 2007–2011, p. 4, internet source.

440 Jämställdhets- och mångfaldspolicy 2009–2011, p. 7, internet source.

441 Mångfaldsplan 2009 för anställda

vid Lunds Universitet, p. 1, internet source.

442 Browne, 2006, p. 90.

443 Jämställdhets- och mångfalds-policy 2009–2011, p. 7, internet source.

444 Koestler, 1954, p. 144.

445 Diskrimineringslag (2008:567), Kap 1, § 5:3, internet source.

446 Friedman, 2007, p. 448.

447 Jämställdhets- och mångfaldspolicy 2009–2011, p. 10–12, internet source.

448 Mångfaldsplan för anställda vid Stockholms universitet 2007–2011, p. 3f, internet source.

449 Strategi och handlingsplan för lika villkor 2012, p. 22, internet source.

450 Ibid., p. 9, internet source.

451 Plan for equal opportunities, University of Linné, 2011.

452 Lasch, 1995, p. 67.

453 Christopher Lasch (just like George Orwell) enters into a similar discussion about the working class in the West. The workers' political attitudes are undeniably more conservative that those of their self-appointed spokespersons and hoped-for liberators. The workers and the lower middle class want to put a limit to abortion, who stick to the nuclear family as a source of stability in a troubled world, and who do not wish any experiments with alternative life styles. (Lasch, 1995, p. 26.) When the indigenous working class emerged as insufficiently progressive and revolutionary, the left instead embraced the ethnic minority, believing that this down-trodden group would offer a new and more handy material in the left's journey towards the future – but seem to have ended up from the ashes into the fire. Sooner or later, the lack of gratitude on the part of the immigrant groups will dawn upon the multicultural left, and the ethnic group will end up next to the worker in the academic trash bin of leftist political abstractions. It is anybody's guess who, then, will be the target of their voluptuously compassionate gaze.

454 Mångfaldsplan 2007–2009 rörande etnisk och social tillhörighet samt religion eller annan tros-uppfattning med åtgärdsprogram för 2009, p. 10, internet source.

455 Ibid.

456 Jämlikhetsplan för Linnéuniversitetet 2011, p. 9, internet source.

457 Mångfaldsplan för anställda vid Stockholms universitet 2007–2011, p. 1, internet source.

458 Adolf Hitler – Mångfaldens fiende. Öppen föreläsning, p. 1, internet source.

459 Malik, debates – can multiculturalism work?, p. 1, internet source.

460 Multiculturalism, Christopher Lasch, claims, evokes a pleasant image of a global bazaar where exotic food, exotic clothes, exotic music and exotic tribal rites can be enjoyed in a big mess without anybody raising their eyebrows and without having to make any commitments'. (Lasch, 1995, p. 9.) Liberal multicultural '"tolerance" condones', Slavoj Žižek maintains, 'the folklorist deprived of its substance – alike the multitude of "ethnic cuisines" in a contemporary megalopolis.' One is tempted, he continues, to reactualize here the old Marcusean notion of repressive tolerance, reconceiving it as the tolerance of the Other in its aseptic, benign form, which forecloses the dimension of the Real of the Other's jouissance. According to Žižek, Erik Kostunica's Underground is a good example of this kind of multicultural jouissance. Underground is (..) the ultimate ideological product of Western liberal multiculturalism: what (it offers) to the

Western liberal gaze is precisely what this gaze wants to see in the Balkan war – the spectacle of a timeless, incomprehensible, mythical cycle of passions, in contrast to decadent and anaemic Western life. A kind of nihilistic kitsch where people make love and kill with the same charming smile on their face. (Žižek, 1997, p. 37f.)

461 Fraser, 1995, p. 68.
462 Ibid., p. 73.
463 Ibid., p. 76.
464 Engels, 1968.
465 Phillips, 1995.
466 Mångfaldsplan för anställda vid Stockholms universitet 2007–2011, p. 1, internet source.
467 Mångfald, p. 1, Lunds Universitet, internet source.
468 Strategi och handlingsplan för lika villkor 2012, p. 9, internet source.
469 Jämställdhets- och mångfaldspolicy 2009–2011, p. 3, internet source.
470 Mångfaldsplan 2009 för anställda vid Lunds Universitet, p. 2, internet source.
471 Mångfaldsplan 2007–2009 rörande etnisk och social tillhörighet samt religion eller annan trosuppfattning med åtgärdsprogram för 2009, p. 4, internet source.
472 Likabehandlingspolicy 2007–2010, p. 2, internet source.
473 Ates, 2007.
474 Žižek, 2007, internet source.
475 Anderson, 2009, p. 530.
476 Lasch, 1995.
477 By Abdel-Samad, see for instance *Mein Abschied vom Himmel: Aus dem Leben eines Muslims in Deutschland*, and *Der Untergang der Islamischen Welt – Eine Prognose*, and by Ayaan Hirsi Ali, see for instance *Nomad – A personal journey through the clash of civilizations*, and *Infidel – My life*.
478 Barry, 2003.
479 Stjernfelt & Eriksen, 2008.
480 Moller Okin, 1999.
481 Hasan, 2009.
482 Merkel, 2010, internet source.
483 Cameron, 2011, internet source.
484 Sarkozy, 2011, internet source.
485 Aznar, 2006, internet source.
486 Suhonen, 2011, internet source.
487 Mångfald i högskolan, p. 3, 127.
488 7.1.4 Rekryteringsfrämjande åtgärder, s. 88, internet source.
489 Eriksen & Stjernfelt, 2008, p. 34.

List of References

Litterature

Abdel-Samad, Hamed, *Mein Abschied vom Himmel: Aus dem Leben eines Muslims in Deutschland*, Knaur, 2010

– *Der Untergang der Islamischen Welt – Eine Prognose*, Knaur, 2010

Adamson, Göran, *Immigrants and Political Participation – Background, Theory, and Empirical Suggestions*, European Union Monitoring Centre on Racism and Xenophobia EUMC, 2002

– *Masochist nationalism – Multicultural self-hatred and the enchantment with the exotic*, Opublicerat manuskript

– *The Spectre of Austria: Reappraising the Rise of the Freedom Party from 1986 to 2000*, London School of Economics and Political Science, 2009

– "Var Jörg Haider rasist?", *Goda sanningar: debattklimatet och den kritiska forskningens villkor*, Nordic Academic Press, 2010

Adamson, Göran; Carlbom, Aje & Ouis, Pernilla, *Herder, Early 19th Century Romanticism, and the Common Roots of Multiculturalism and Right-wing Populism*, Telos Press, 2014

Alba, R. & Nee, V. *Remaking the American Mainstream: Assimilation and Contemporary Immigration*, Harvard University Press, 2003

Alesina, A; Baqir, R & Easterly, W., 'Public Goods and Ethnic Divisions', *Quarterly Journal of Economics* 114, 1999, s. 1243–1284.

Alesina, A. & La Farrara, E., "Participation in Heterogeneous Communities", *Quarterly Journal of Economics* 115, 2000, s. 847–904

– "Who Trusts Others?", *Journal of Public Economics* 85, 2002, s. 207–234

Alvesson, Mats & Sveningsson, Stefan, *Organisationer, ledning och processer*, Lund: Studentlitteratur, 2012

Alvesson, Mats, *Tomhetens triumf: om grandiositet, illusionsnummer & nollsummespel*, Stockholm: Atlas, 2006

Andersson, C. J. & Paskeviciute, A., "How Ethnic and Linguistic Heterogeneity Influence the Prospects for Civic Society: A Comparative Study of Citizenship Behavior", *Journal of Politics* 68, 2006, s. 783–802

Andersson, Roger, "Segregationens Sverige", *Invandrarskap och medborgarskap – dokumentation från ett seminarium,* Demokratiutredningens skrift, Nr. 13, 1999

Anderson, Perry, *The New Old World*, London: Verso, 2009

Appiah, K. A., "Identitet, autenticitet, överlevnad" Taylor, Charles, *Det mångkulturella samhället och erkännandets politik,* Göteborg, Daidalos, 1995

Asante, Molefi, "An Afrocentric Curriculum", *Educational Leadership 49*, Nr. 4, Dec. 1991–Jan. 1992

Ates, Seyran, *Der Multikulti-Irrtum – Wie wir in Deutschland besser zusammenleben können*, Berlin: Ullstein, 2007

Banner-Haley, C.P., "We Can't Go Home Again: An Argument about Afrocentrism", *Journal of Southern History*, Vol 69 (3), 2003

Barry, Brian, *Culture and Equality: An Egalitarian Critique of Multiculturalism,* Cambridge MA: Harvard University Press, 2001

Bauman, Zygmunt, *Community; Seeking Safety in an Insecure World,* Malden: Blackwell, 2001

Bawer, Bruce, *While Europe Slept – How Radical Islam is Destroying the West from within*, New York: Doubleday, 2006

Bech Dyrberg, Torben, "Identitetspolitisk offerideologi og hykleri – om venstreorientering i dag", *Kritik*, Köpenhamn, 2008

Bech, Henning & Ümit Necef, Mehmet, *Er danskerne racister? Invandrerforskningens problemer,* Frederiksberg: Frydenlund, 2013

Berlin, Isaiah, Hardy, Henry & Hausheer, Roger (utg.), *The Proper Study of Mankind – An Anthology of Ideas. Isaiah Berlin,* London: Pimlico, 1998

Betz, Hans-Georg, "The Enigmatic Haider", i *SAIS Review*, Washington: Johns Hopkins School of Advanced International Studies, Vol. 20:2, Sommar-Höst, 2000, s. 265–271

Black, Jeffrey H. & Lakhani, Aleem S., "Ethnoracial Diversity in the House of Commons: An Analysis of Numerical Representation in the 35th Parliament", *Canadian Ethnic Studies*, November, 1997

Blalock, H. M. Jr., *Towards a Theory of Minority-Group Relations*, New York: John Wiley & Sons, 1967
Blumer, H., "Race Prejudices as a Sense of Group Position", *Pacific Sociological Review 1*, 1958, s. 3–7
Bobbio, Norberto, *Left and Right: The Significance of a Political Distinction,* Cambridge: Polity Press, 1995
Bobo L. D., "Prejudice as Group Position: Microfoundations of a Sociological Approach to Racism and Race Relations", *Journal of Social Issues* 55, 1999, s. 445–472
Bobo L. D. & Tuan, M., *Prejudice in Politics: Group Position, Public Opinion and the Wisconson Treaty Rights Dispute*, Cambridge, MA: Harvard University Press, 2006
Bourdieu, Pierre, *Moteld – Texter mot nyliberalismens utbredning*, Stockholm/Stehag: Brutus Östling Bokförlag, 2000
Brewer, M. B. & Brown, R. J., "Intergroup Relations", Gilbert, D. T; Fiske, S. T. & Lindzey, G. (utg.), *Handbook of Social Psychology* 4/98, New York: Oxford University Press, 1998
Browne, Anthony, *The Retreat of Reason: Political Correctness and the Corruption of Public Debate in Modern Britain,* London: Civitas, 2006
Caldwell, Christopher, *Reflections on the Revolution in Europe: Immigration, Islam and the West,* New York: Anchor Books, 2010
Canovan, Margaret, *Hannah Arendt: A Reinterpretation of her Political Thought,* Cambridge: Cambridge University Press, 1992
Carlbom, Aje, *The Imagined versus the Real Other – Multiculturalism and the Representation of Muslims in (Sic!) Sweden*, Lund: Dept. of Sociology, Lund University, 2003
Charles, K. & Kline, P., *Relations Costs and the Production of Social Capital: Evidence from Carpooling,* Cambridge MA: National Bureau Economic Research, NBER Working Paper 9041, 2002
Cohen, Nick, *What's Left – How the Left Lost its Way,* London: Harper Perennial, 2007
Cohen, S. G. & Bailey, D. E., "What Makes Teams Work: Group Effectiveness Research from the Shop Floor to the Executive Suite", *Journal of Management* 23, 1997, s. 239–290

Costa, D. L & Kahn, M. E., "Civic Engagement and Community Heterogeneity: An Economists Perspective", *Perspectives on Politics 1*, 2003, s. 103–111
Crick, Bernhard, *In Defence of Politics,* Harmondsworth: Penguin, 1984
Cwejman, Adam, *Välviljans rasism,* Stockholm: Timbro, 2012
Danneskiold-Samsøe, Sofie; Mørck, Yvonne & Wagner Sørensen, Bo, *'Familien betyder alt' – Vold mod kvinder i etniske minoritetsfamilier,* Frederiksberg: Frydenlund, 2011
Demirbag-Sten, Dilsa & Bauhn, Per, *Till frihetens försvar: en kritik av den normativa multikulturalismen,* Stockholm: Norstedt, 2010
Dostojevskij, Fjodor, *Anteckningar från ett källarhål,* Falun: Atlantis, 1985
Durkheim, Émile, *On Suicide,* New York: Penguin Books, 2006
Engels, Friedrich, *The Condition of the Working-class in England in 1844,* London: Allen & Unwin, 1968
Eriksen, Jens Martin & Stjernfelt, Frederik, *Adskillelsens politik: multikulturalisme – ideologi og virkelighed,* Köpenhamn: Lindhardt og Ringhof, 2008
Eriksson, R. & Jonsson, J., *Ursprung och utbildning, SOU 1993:85,* Stockholm: Allmänna förlaget, 1993
Falsafi, Leili, *På tal om mångfald,* Stockholm: Natur och Kultur, 2004
Finkelstein, Norman G., *The Holocaust Industry: Reflections on the Exploitation of Jewish Suffering,* London: Verso, 2000
Flyvbjerg, Bent, "Five Misunderstandings About Case-Study Research", *Qualitative Inquiry,* Sage Publications, Vol. 12, Nr. 2, April 2006, s. 219–245
Fraser, N., "From Redistribution to Recognition? Dilemmas of Justice in a 'Post-Socialist' Age", *New Left Review,* no. 212, July/August, 1995
Friedman, Jonathan, "Champagne Liberals and the New "Dangerous Classes" – Reconfigurations of Class, Identity and Cultural Production in the Contemporary Global System", *Social Analysis,* Berghahn Books, Vol. 46, Nr. 2, Sommar 2002

– ”Cosmopolitan Elites, Organic Intellectuals and the Re-configuration of the State”, Kouvouama Abel et al (utg.) *Figures croisées d'intellectuels. Trajectoires, modes d'action, productions*, Paris: Karthala, 2007
– ”Power, Pluralism and the Transformation of Governance in an Era of Declining Hegemony”, Pansters, Wil G., (utg.), *The Troubled Triangle: Unravelling the Linkages Between Inequality, Pluralism and Environment*, Amsterdam: Rozenberg Publishers, 2009
Gerle, Elisabeth, *Mångkulturalism för vem?*, Nora: Nya Doxa, 1999
Giles M. W. & Evans, A., "The Power Approach to Intergroup Hostility", *Journal of Conflict Resolution* 30, 1986, s. 469–485
Glaeser E. & Alesina, A., *Fighting Poverty in the US and Europe: A World of Difference,* Oxford: Oxford University Press, 2004
Golsan, Richard, *Fascism's Return: Scandal, Revision and Ideologi Since 1980,* Lincoln: University of Nebraska Press, 1998
Haider, Jörg, *Befreite Zukunft jenseits von links und rechts: Menschliche Alternativen für eine Brücke ins neue Jahrtausend,* Vienna: Ibera, 1997
Hasan, Rumy, *Multiculturalism – Some Inconvenient Truths*, London: Politico' s, 2010
Hayek, Friedrich, *Individualism and Economic Order*, Chicago: University of Chicago Press, 1948
– *Law, Legislation and Liberty*, *3* volymer, London: Routledge, 1973/1998
Hirsi Ali, Ayaan, *Nomad – A Personal Journey Through the Clash of Civilizations,* London: Simon and Schuster, 2010
– *Infidel – My life,* London: Simon and Schuster, 2007
Hooghe, M., et al. "Ethnic Diversity, Trust and Ethnocentrism and Europe: A multilevel Analysis of 21 European Countries", Unpublished Paper presented at American Political Science Association Annual Meeting, 2006
Hummer, Waldemar & Pelinka, Anton, Österreich unter ”EU-Quarantäne”: Die ”Masshahmen der 14” gegen die österreichische Bundesregierung aus politikwissenschaftlicher und juristischer Sicht. *Chronologie, Kommentare,*

Dokumentation, Wien: Linde Verlag, 2002
Hylland Eriksen, Thomas, *Kulturterrorismen: En uppgörelse med tanken om kulturell renhet,* Nora: Nya Doxa, 1999
Jackson S., et al, "Some Difference Make a Difference: Individual Dissimilarity and Group Heterogeneity as Correlates of Recruitment, Promotions and Turnover", *Journal of Applied Psychology* 76, 1991, s. 675–689
Jordahl, H & Gustavsson, M., *Inequality and Trust in Sweden: Some Inequalities are More Harmful than Others*, Stockholm: Ratio, Radio Working Paper 106, 2006
Keller, R. T., "Cross-Functional Project Groups in Research and New Product Development: Diversity, Communication, Job Stress and Outcomes", *Academy of Management Journal* 44, 2001, s. 547–555
Koestler, Arthur, *Den osynliga skriften,* Stockholm: Tiden, 1954
Kommittédirektiv Social och etnisk mångfald i högskolan, Beslut vid regeringssammanträde den 21 oktober 1999. Sammanfattning av uppdraget, Bilaga 1 Dir., 1999:79, Sveriges riksdag
Kowalsky, Wolfgang, *Rechtsaussen… und die verfehlten Strategien der deutschen Linken*, Frankfurt/M: Ullstein, 1992
Kowalsky, Wolfgang & Schroeder, Wolfgang (utg.), *Rechtsextremismus – Einführung und Forschungsbilanz*, Opladen: Westdeutscher Verlag, 1994
Laqueur, Walter, *After the Fall – The End of the European Dream,* New York: Thomas Dunne Books/St. Martin's Press, 2011
Lasch, Christopher, *Eliternas Uppror – och sveket mot demokratin,* Stockholm: SNS, 1995
– *The Revolt of the Elites and the Betrayal of Democracy*, New York and London: W. W. Norton & Company, 1995
Leigh, A, "Trust, Inequality and Ethnic Heterogeneity", *Economic Record 82*, 2006, s. 268–280
Lundquist, Lennart, *Slutet på yttrandefriheten (och demokratin?),* Stockholm: Carlsson Bokförlag, 2012
Löfgren, Eva & Wadstein, Margareta, *Aktiva åtgärder för att främja etnisk mångfald i arbetslivet*, Ombudsmannen mot etnisk diskriminering, 1999

Malik, Kenan, *From Fatwa to Jihad: The Rushdie Affair and its Aftermath,* New York: Melville, 2010
Mannheim, K., *Ideology and Utopia,* London: Routledge, 1936
Moller Okin, S., *Is multiculturalism Bad for Women?,* Princeton N.J.: Princeton University Press, 1999
Newton, K & Delhey, J., "Predicting Cross-National Levels of Social Trust: Global Pattern or Nordic Exceptionalism?" *European Sociological Review,* 2005, s. 311–327
O'Reilly, C.; Williams, R. K. & Barsage, S., "Group Demography and Innovation: Does Diversity Help?" i Mannix, E. & Neale, M. (utg.), *Research in Managing Groups and Teams,* Vol 1, Greenwich CT: JAI Press, 1997, s. 183–207.
Orwell, George, *The Road to Wigan Pier,* London: Penguin, 2001
Page, Scott, *The Difference: How the Power of Diversity Creates Better Groups, Firms, Schools and Societies,* Princeton, NJ: Princeton University Press, 2007
Pennant, R., *Diversity, Trust, and Community Participation in England,* Home Office Findings 253, Research, Development and Statistics Directorate, London, 2005
Phillips, Anne, *The Politics of Presence,* Oxford, New York: Clarendon Press, 1995
Poterba, J. M., "Demographic Structure and the Political Economy of Public Education", *Journal of Policy Analysis and Management* 16, 1997, s. 48–66
Prasad, P & Prasad, A, "Diversity by Design: Managing Diversity and the Discourse of Fashion", Working paper, Saratoga Springs, NY, USA: Skidmore College, 2004
Putnam, Robert D., *E Pluribus Unum: Diversity and Community in the Twenty-first Century, Scandinavian Political Studies,* Nordic Political Science Association, Vol. 30, No. 2, 2007
Quillian, L., "Prejudice as a Response to Perceived Group Threat: Population Composition and Anti-Immigrant and Racial Prejudice in Europe", *American Sociological Review* 60, 1995, s. 586–611
– "Group Threat and Regional Change in Attitudes Towards African Americans", *American Journal of Sociology* 102, 1996,

s. 816-60
Rawls, John, *A Theory of Justice,* London and Cambridge MA: Belknap Press, 1971
Reuterberg, Sven-Erik, "Etnisk bakgrund och högskoleprovet", *Fokus på Högskoleprovet,* Stockholm: Högskoleverket, 1999
Riedlsperger, Max, "The FPÖ and the Right", Günther Bischof och Anton Pelinka (utg.), *Austro Corporatism – Past, Present, Future,* New Brunswick, NJ: Transaction Publishers, 1996, s. 351–367
Roth, Hans Ingvar, *Mångfaldens gränser,* Stockholm: Arena, 1996
Scruton, Roger, *The West and the Rest: Globalization and the Terrorist Threat,* Wilmington, DE: ISI Books, 2002
– T*he Uses of Pessimism: And the Danger of False Hope,* Oxford: Oxford University Press, 2010
Serge, Victor, *Memoirs of a Revolutionary,* London: Writers and Readers, 1984
Simonton, D. K., *Origins of Genius,* New York: Oxford University Press, 1999
Soroka, S. N.; Helliwell, J. F. & Johnston, R., "Measuring and Modeling Interpersonal Trust", F. M. Kay och R. Johnston (utg.), *Social Capital, Diversity and the Welfare State,* Vancouver: UBC Press, 2007
Steyn, Mark, *America Alone: The End of the World As We Know it,* Washington: Regnery, 2006
Stouffer, S., *American Soldier,* Princeton, NJ: Princeton University Press, 1949
Suhonen, Daniel, "En rutten röra", Sydsvenskan, 30 dec. 2011
Sörensen, J. S., "The Return of Plural Society: Statebuilding and Social Splintering", *Journal of Peacebuilding,* 2014.
Taggart, Paul, *Populism, Concepts in the Social Science,* Buckingham, Philadelphia: Open University Press, 2000
Taylor, M., "Local Racial/Ethnic Proportions and White Attitudes: Numbers Count", *American Sociological Review* 63, 1998, s. 512–535
Thormark, Catarina, "Studenter och lärare måste samarbeta", *Universitetsläraren,* Stockholm: SULF, 7/2013

Trägårdh, Lars; Wallman Lundåsen, Susanne; Wollebæck, Dag & Svedberg, Lars, *Den svala svenska tilliten. Förutsättningar och utmaningar*, Stockholm: SNS förlag, 2013
Vigdor, J. L., "Community Composition and Collective Action: Analyzing Initial Mail Response to the 2000 Census", *Review of Economics and Statistics* 86, 2004, s. 303–312
Webber, S. S. & Donahue, L. M., "Impact of Highly and Less Job-related Diversity on Work Group Cohesion and Performance: A Meta–analysis", *Journal of Management* 27, s. 141–162, 2001
Webster, Yehudi O., *Against the Multicultural Agenda – A Critical Thinking alternative*, Westport, Connecticut & London: Praeger, 1997
Wild, wild, West, Movie, 1999
Williams, K. Y. & O' Reilly, C. A., "Demography and Diversity in Organizations: A Review of 40 Years of Research", Staw, B. M. & Cummings L. L. (utg.), *Research in Organizational Behavior*, Vol. 20, Greenwich, CT: JAI Press, 1998
Wood, Peter, *Diversity – The Invention of a Concept*, San Francisco, California: Encounter Books, 2003
Žižek, Slavoj, "Multiculturalism, Or, the Cultural Logic of Multinational Capitalism", *New Left Review*, London, I/225, Sept-Okt, 1997
– *The Ticklish Subject: The Absent Centre of Political Ontology*, London: Verso, 1999
– "Why We All Love to Hate Haider", *New Left Review*, Vol. 2, 2000

Internet

"7.1.4 Rekryteringsfrämjande åtgärder, Kap. 16 Utbildning och universitetsforskning", i *Budgetpropositionen för 2002, Prop. 2001/02:1*, Stockholm: Finansdepartementet, tillgänglig på: http://www.regeringen.se/content/1/c4/31/36/2e0d4d2d.pdf, citerad 2012-07-02
"Adolf Hitler – Mångfaldens fiende. Öppen föreläsning", *Malmö*

Högskola, 20/10-2010, tillgänglig på: http://www.mah.se/Nyheter/Nyheter-2010/Adolf-Hitler--mangfaldens-fiende/, citerad 2012-05-30
A guide to European diversity, available at: https://www.salto-youth.net/downloads/4-17-973/SALTO%20 booklet_new.pdf, cited 2014-10-15
"Ambassadörer arbetar för mångfald", *Lundagård.se*, tillgänglig på: http://lundagard.se/2010/04/23/ambassadorer-arbetar-for-mangfald/, citerad 2012-05-30
"Ansvarsfull invandringspolitik", *Sverigedemokraterna*, tillgänglig på: https://sverigedemokraterna.se/vara-asikter/vara-viktigaste-fragor/ansvarsfull-invandringspolitik/, citerad 2012-05-30
Approach to cultural diversity in Italy, available at: http://www.adam-europe.eu/prj/8820/prj/R5%20-%20Report%20Cultural%20Diversity%20ITALY.pdf, cited 2014-10-15
Aznar, José María, "Multiculturalism is a Big failure", tillgänglig på: http://www.abigmessage.com/multiculturalism-a-failure-in-germany-uk-spain-france-and-australia-but-thriving-in-canada.html, citerad 2013-01-12
'BBC – Everyone has a story. The BBC's Dversity Strategy 2011-15', available at: http://downloads.bbc.co.uk/diversity/pdf/Diversity_strategy_110523.pdf, cited 2014-10-14
Begreppet invandrare – användningen i myndigheters verksamhet (Ds 2000:43, tillgänglig på: http://www.regeringen.se/content/1/c4/18/78/6e54e14b.pdf, citerad 2012-05-30
"Bernard Crick", tillgänglig på: http://en.wikipedia.org/wiki/Bernard_Crick, citerad 2013-01-13
Bortom Multikulti. Konferens, Engelsbergs Bruk, Västmanland, 13 April, 2011, tillgänglig på: http://www.axsonjohnsonfoundation.org/Bortom-Multikulti.pdf
Cameron, David, "State multiculturalism has failed, says David Cameron", tillgänglig på: http://www.bbc.co.uk/news/uk-politics-12371994, citerad 2013-01-12
'Canadian Multiculturalism: An Inclusive Citizenship', available at: http://www.cic.gc.ca/english/multiculturalism/citizenship.asp, cited 2014-10-15 The Challenge of French Diversity, available at:

file:///Users/user/Documents/The%20Challenge%20of%20French%20Diversity%20%7C%20migrationpolicy.org.webarchive, cited 2014-10-15
Diskrimineringslag, 2008:567, Kap 1, ”Inledande bestämmelser”; § 5 ”Kön, könsöverskridande identitet eller uttryck, etnisk tillhörighet, funktionshinder, sexuell läggning och ålder”; 3. etnisk tillhörighet: nationellt eller etniskt ursprung, hudfärg eller annat liknande förhållande, tillgänglig på: http://www.notisum.se/rnp/sls/lag/20080567.htm, citerad 2012-07-15
Diversity charters across the EU, available at: http://ec.europa.eu/justice/discrimination/diversity/charters/index_en.htm, cited 2014-10-15. Does TV Capture the Diversity of America Yet?, available at: file:///Users/user/Documents/Does%20TV%20Capture%20the%20Diversity%20of%20America%20Yet%3F%20-%20WorldNews.webarchive, cited 2014-10-14
”EDA – european diversity awards”, available at: http://europeandiversityawards.com/about-the-eda/, cited 2014-10-15
”En resa in i framtiden, Strategi 2010-2015, Linnéuniversitetet”, tillgänglig på: http://lnu.se/polopoly_fs/1.10921!LNU-strategi_sve.pdf, citerad 2013-06-21
”Etnicitet, mångfald och integration 7.5 hp”, tillgänglig på: http://sisu.it.su.se/info/SOE110, citerad 2012-06-25
”Etnisk mångfald”, *Lunds Universitet*, tillgänglig på: http://www5.lu.se/o.o.i.s/40, citerad 2012-05-30
”Etnisk och kulturell mångfald”, *Kulturrådet*, 2012, tillgänglig på: http://www.kulturradet.se/sv/verksamhet/Kulturell-mangfald/, citerad 2012-05-30
”Ett inkluderande universitet – en handlingsplan för likabehandling, tillgänglighet och mångfald för studenter och anställda 2007-2010”, *Umeå Universitet*, tillgänglig på: http://www.student.umu.se/digitalAssets/23/23568_inkluderande_universitet.pdf, citerad 2012-09-06
Fredriksson, Daniel, ”Mångfald berikar”, Kristdemokraterna, *Nutidningen – Finnveden, Jönköping, Höglandet*, Dec. 2011, tillgänglig på: http://www.nutidningen.nu/index.php/debatt/102-familje-jnu/18319-Maangfald-berikar, citerad 2012-05-30

”Fremde Kulturen im europäischen Fernsehen”, available at: file:///Users/user/Documents/Fremde%20Kulturen%20im%20 europäischen%20Fernsehen%20-%20Zur%20Thematik%20 der%20fremden%20Kulturen%20in%20den%20Fernsehprogramm.webarchive, cited 2014-10-15
French Diversity Charter, available at: http://www.diversity-charter.com/diversity-charter-commitment.php, cited 2014-10-15
”French National Front's black and Arab supporters”, internet source. file:///Users/user/Documents/BBC%20News%20 -%20French%20National%20Front's%20black%20and%20 Arab%20supporters.webarchive, cited 2014-10-15
Förbundet Liberal Mångfald – Liberal Mångfald, 2012, tillgänglig på: http://www.folkpartiet.se/Vi-behover-dig/Engagera-dig-i-ett-natverk/Forbundet-Liberal-Mangfald/, citerad 2012-05-30
”Församlingsinstruktion för Stora Tuna och Torsångs församlingar – Svenska Kyrkan i Borlänge”, tillgänglig på: http://www.svenskakyrkan.se/default.aspx?id=894101, citerad 2013-01-18
”Handlingsplaner för breddad rekrytering, 7.2.2 Rekrytering och tillträde till högre utbildning, Kap. 16 Utbildning och universitetsforskning”, *Budgetpropositionen för 2007, Prop-2006/07:1*, s. 143, tillgänglig på: http://www.regeringen.se/content/1/c6/06/96/26/39fffe85.pdf, citerad 2012-07-03
”Heliga danser för mångfald, rättvisa och hållbarhet (32)”, *Svenska Kyrkan*, tillgänglig på: http://www.svenskakyrkan.se/default.aspx?id=867046, citerad 2012-05-30
”Högskolor och universitet i Sverige”, *Wikipedia*, tillgänglig på: http://sv.wikipedia.org/wiki/H%c3%b6gskolor_och_universitet_i_Sverige, citerad 2012-05-30
”Innovation genom mångfald när nya svenska möter landsbygden”, *Jordbruksverket*, 2012-03-12, tillgänglig på: http://www.jordbruksverket.se/formedier/nyheter/nyheter2012/innovationgenommangfaldnarnyasvenskarmoterlandsbygden.5.13af5402136oocc8df7a8000205.htm, citerad 2012-05-30
”Integration och mångfald”, *Socialdemokraterna*, tillgänglig på: http://www.socialdemokraterna.se/Var-politik/Var-politik-A-till-O/Integration/, citerad 2012-05-30

"Integration", *Regeringskansliet*, tillgänglig på: http://www.regeringen.se/sb/d/2279?setEnableCookies=trueUD, citerad 2012-05-30
"Italy Gives Cultural Diversity a Lukewarm Embrace", available at: http://www.nytimes.com/2008/06/25/arts/design/25abroad.html?pagewanted=all&_r=0, cited 2014-10-15
"Jämlikhetsplan för Linnéuniversitetet 2011, Dnr 2011/112", *Linnéuniversitetet*, 2011, tillgänglig på: http://lnu.se/polopoly_fs/1.63069!Jamlikhetsplan.pdf, citerad 2012-07-15
"Jämställdhets- och mångfaldspolicy 2009–2011. Enligt Diskrimineringslagen, SFS 2008:567", *Malmö Högskola*, tillgänglig på: http://www.mah.se/upload/Gemensam%2f%c3%b6rvaltning/dokument_mah/Jamstalldhets-mangfaldspolicy-090604.pdf, citerad 2013-01-18
"Kandidatprogram i Equality and Diversity Management 180.0 hp.", *Lunds Universitet*, tillgänglig på: http://www.lu.se/o.o.i.s?id=320&lukas_id=SGMFU, citerad 2012-05-30
Karlskoga Folkhögskola, tillgänglig på: http://www.hittaskola.se/index.php/BrowseSchool/index/53979, citerad 2012-05-30
Kommittédirektiv – Social och etnisk mångfald i högskolan, Dir. 1999:79, tillgänglig på: http://www.riksdagen.se/sv/Dokument-Lagar/Utredningar/Kommittedirektiv/_DIR1999;79/?text=true, citerad 2012-05-30
"Kulturkalendern – Din kulturmötesplats", tillgänglig på: http://www.vaxjopuls.se/kulturkalendern?eid=849, citerad 2013-01-13.
"Krönika: Den radikala kampmetoden är den enda rätta!", tillgänglig på: http://www.nationell.nu/2013/01/16/kronika-den-radikala-kampmetoden-ar-den-enda-ratta/, citerad 2013-03-28
"Likabehandlingspolicy 2007–2010", *Göteborgs Universitet*, tillgänglig på: http://www.styrdokument.adm.gu.se/digitalAssets/1293/1293628_Policylikabehandling091218.pdf, citerad 2012-07-15
"Linköpings Universitets arbete med social och etnisk mångfald", 2003-04-16, tillgänglig på: http://www.liu.se/om-liu/strategi/kvalitet/hsvutvarderingar/1.29899/mangfald.pdf, citerad 2012-05-30
Malik, Kenan, *debates – can multiculturalism work?* tillgänglig på:

http://www.kenanmalik.com/lectures/multiculturalism_if.html, citerad 2012-05-30
"Masterprogram i intersektionalitetsstudier, 120 hp", tillgänglig på: http://sisu.it.su.se/search/info/SISSO, citerad 2012-06-25
Merkel, Angela, "Merkel erklärt multikulti für gescheitert", tillgänglig på: http://www.spiegel.de/politik/deutschland/integration-merkel-erklaert-multikulti-fuer-gescheitert-a-723532.html, citerad 2013-01-12
'Mission' – Organisation for Friendship in Diversity (OFD, Malta), available at: http://ofd.org.mt/about/vision/, cited 2014-10-15
"MP: Vi har en härlig mångfald", *ekuriren, Eskilstunakuriren på nätet*, 2010-09-19, tillgänglig på: http://ekuriren.se/val2010/1.812188-mp-vi-har-en-harlig-mangfald, citerad 2012-05-30
"Multiculturalism is communism", *Faith & Heritage*, tillgänglig på: http://faithandheritage.com/2012/06/multiculturalism-is-communism/, citerad 2013-04-01
Myndigheters mångfaldsarbete. Kartläggning inför utvärderingen av ett regionalt utvecklingsprojekt, tillgänglig på: http://www.statskontoret.se/upload/Publikationer/2007/200701.pdf, citerad 2012-05-30
"Måldokument 2010", *Göteborgs Universitet*, tillgänglig på: http://www.gu.se/digitalAssets/103/103629_gbg_universitet_2010.pdf, citerad 2012-05-30
Mångfald berikar – Kristdemokraterna", *Nutidningen*, tillgänglig på: http://www.nutidningen.nu/index.php/debatt/102-familjejnu/18319-Maangfald-berikar, citerad 2012-07-15
"Mångfald – framgångsfaktor för hållbar tillväxt" – *Nya Malmömoderaterna*, tillgänglig på: http://malmömoderaterna.se/2011/09/29/mangfald-framgangsfaktor-for-hallbar-tillvaxt/, citerad 2012-05-30
"Mångfald – Ger mervärde och affärsnytta", *Diversity Group*, tillgänglig på: http://www.diversitygroup.se/politiker-om-mangfald/, citerad 2012-07-15
Mångfald i högskolan – reflektioner och förslag om social och etnisk mångfald i högskolan, SOU 2000:47, tillgänglig på: http://www.

regeringen.se/content/1/c4/12/20/ecf91dd4.pdf, citerad 2012-05-30
”Mångfald”, *Lunds Universitet*, tillgänglig på: http://www4.lu.se/o.o.i.s/526, citerad 2013-01-18
”Mångfald och likvärdighet – Skolans värdegrund”, *Skolverket*, tillgänglig på: http://www.skolverket.se/skolutveckling/vardegrund/allas_lika_varde/2.2357, citerad 2013-01-18
”Mångfald”, *Polisen i Stockholms län*, tillgänglig på: http://www.polisen.se/Om-polisen/lan/St/op/Polisen-i-Stockholms-lan/Brottsutredning/Test-Polisarbete-med-HBT-och-hatbrott/mangfald/, citerad 2013-01-18
”Mångfaldskonsulent”, tillgänglig på: http://www.google.com/search?client=safari&rls=en&q=Mångfaldskonsulent&ie=UTF-8&oe=UTF-8, citerad 2012-05-30
”Mångfaldskonsult”, tillgänglig på: http://www.google.com/search?client=safari&rls=en&q=mångfaldskonsult&ie=UTF-8&oe=UTF-8
”Mångfaldsplan 2007–2009 rörande etnisk och social tillhörighet samt religion eller annan trosuppfattning med åtgärdsprogram för 2009”, *Uppsala Universitet*, tillgänglig på: http://www.ucrs.uu.se/digitalAssets/6/6670_m_ngfaldsplan2009.pdf, citerad 2014-01-15
”Mångfaldsplan 2009 för anställda vid Lunds Universitet”, tillgänglig på: http://www3.lu.se/pers/Mangfald/mangfaldsplan_2009.pdf, citerad 2012-05-30
”Mångfaldsplan för anställda vid Stockholms universitet 2007–2011”, *Personalbyrån*. tillgänglig på: http://www.su.se/polopoly_fs/1.24243.1316519474!/menu/standard/file/Mangfaldsplan_2007_06_18.pdf, citerad 2012-05-30
”Mångfaldspolicy för Växjö Universitet 2003”, tillgänglig på: http://www.hsv.se/download/18.5b73fe55111705b51fd80006519/V%C3%A4xj%C3%B6+universitet.pdf, citerad 2012-07-13
”Mångfald”, tillgänglig på: http://www.lu.se/om-lunds-universitet/policydokument-och-planer/maangfald, citerad 2012-05-30
”Mångfaldsveckan: Låna en forskare på högskolan Väst”, tillgänglig på: http://sverigesradio.se/sida/artikel.aspx?programid=125&artikel=2427251, citerad 2013-01-13

”Mångfaldsvecka på högskolan i Skövde”, tillgänglig på: http://www.studentum.se/Sections/Newsdesk/Newsdesk.aspx?NewsdeskID=284, citerad 2013-01-13
”Nationaldemokraterna – Våra viktigaste frågor”, tillgänglig på: http://www.nd.se/vara-viktigaste-fragor, citerad 2013-03-28
”Nordfront – Det fria Nordens röst”, tillgänglig på: http://www.nordfront.se/jamlikhet-utveckling-radikal-dialektik-och-skapandet-av-overmanniskan.smr, citerad 2013-03-28
Orwell, George, *Notes on Nationalism*, tillgänglig på: http://orwell.ru/library/essays/nationalism/english/e_nat, citerad 2012-05-30
Pennant, R., *Diversity, Trust, and Community Participation in England*, Home Office Findings 253, Research, Development and Statistics Directorate., 2005, tillgänglig på: http://www.blink.org.uk/does/ho_findings_diversity-trust.pdf, citerad 2012-05-30
”Perspektivområden”, Malmö Högskola, tillgänglig på: http://www.mah.se/Om-Malmo-hogskola/fakta-statistik/Perspektivomraden/, citerad 2013-01-25
Persson, Anders, ”Från utredning till opinionsbildning”, *FLS-Aktuellt*, Nr 1, 2001, tillgänglig på: https://lup.lub.lu.se/luur/download?func=downloadFile&recordOId=707463&fileOId=1299437, citerad 2012-05-30
”Pluralism i Mångfald”, *Högskolan i Väst*, tillgänglig på: http://www.hv.se/extra/pod/?action=pod_show&id=66&module_instance=1&url=http%3A%2F%2Fwww.hv.se%3A80%2Fextra%2Fnews%2F%3Fmodule_instance%3D1%26id%3D6567, citerad 2012-05-30
”Rasismens olika ansikten – Skolans värdegrund”, *Skolverket*, tillgänglig på: http://www.skolverket.se/skolutveckling/vardegrund/allas_lika_varde/2.2357/rasismens-olika-ansikten-1.140071, citerad 2012-05-30
”Regleringsbrev för Budgetåret 2008 avseende Statens Haverikommission”, 18/12-2008, tillgänglig på: http://www.esv.se/Verktyg--stod/Statsliggaren/Regleringsbrev/?RBID=11218, citerad 2012-05-30
”Rosengård ska krydda Sverige”, SDS, *Sydsvenskan*, tillgänglig på:

http://www.sydsvenskan.se/ekonomi/ekonomi-lordag/rosengard-ska-krydda-sverige/, citerad 2013-01-26
Sarkozy, Nicolas, "Nicolas Sarkozy joins David Cameron and Angela Merkel view that multiculturalism has failed", tillgänglig på: http://www.dailymail.co.uk/news/article-1355961/Nicolas-Sarkozy-joins-David-Cameron-Angela-Merkel-view-multiculturalism-failed.html, citerad 2013-01-12
"Sex personer gripna i Kina efter rykten om statskupp", *DN.se*, 2012-03-31, tillgänglig på: http://www.dn.se/nyheter/varlden/sex-personer-gripna-i-kina-efter-rykten-om-statskupp, citerad 2013-01-18
"Sjuksköterskeprogrammet", *Malmö Högskola*, tillgänglig på: http://www.edu.mah.se/VGSSK/syllabus/, citerad 2012-05-30
"Socionomprogrammet – Inriktning funktionshinder och åldrande", *Malmö Högskola*, tillgänglig på: http://www.edu.mah.se/SGSOF/syllabus/, citerad 2012-05-30
"Socionomprogrammet – Inriktning individ, familj och samhälle", *Malmö Högskola*, tillgänglig på: http://www.edu.mah.se/SGSOI/syllabus/, citerad 2012-05-30
"Socionomprogrammet – Inriktning verksamhetsutveckling", *Malmö Högskola*, tillgänglig på: http://www.edu.mah.se/SGSOV/syllabus/, citerad 2012-05-30
'Spain implements a practical approach to managing diversity!' – Council of Europé, available at: file:///Users/user/Documents/Spain%20implements%20a%20practical%20approach%20to%20managing%20diversity!.webarchive, cited 2014-10-15
Stasiulis, Daiva, K., "Participation by Immigrants, Ethnocultural/visible Minorities in the Canadian Political Process", *Second National Metropolis Conference, Immigrants and Civic Participation*: Contemporary Policy and Research Issues, Montréal, 1997, tillgänglig på: http://canada.metropolis.net/events/civic/dstasiulis_e.html, citerad 2012-05-30
"Strategi och handlingsplan för lika villkor 2012", *Linköpings universitet*, tillgänglig på: http://www.liu.se/om-liu/strategi/ett-liu-for-alla/lika-villkor/filarkiv/1.316628/HP_2012.pdf, s. 3, citerad 2012-05-30

Suhonen, Daniel, ”En rutten röra”, *Sydsvenskan*, tillgänglig på: http://www.sydsvenskan.se/kultur--nojen/en-rutten-rora/, citerad 2013-06-22
‘Survey on cultural diversity’, internet source, available at: file:///Users/user/Documents/Survey%20on%20cultural%20diversity%20-%20timesofmalta.com.webarchive, cited 2014-10-15
”Svart tjej i toppen för Sveriges Radio”, tillgänglig på: http://www.uppmana.nu/nyheter-arbetsmarknad/4799-svart-tjej-i-toppen-fveriges-radio, citerad 2013-01-13
‘Teachers Initial Training in Cultural Diversity in Spain: Attitudes and Pedagogical Strategies’, available at: file:///Users/user/Documents/ERIC%20-%20Teachers’%20Initial%20Training%20in%20Cultural%20Diversity%20in%20Spain:%20Attitudes%20and%20Pedagogical%20Strategi.webarchive, cited 2014-10-15
”Umgang mit Migrantinnen und Migranten – Multikulturalismus in Kanada – Modell für Deutschland?”, available at: file:///Users/user/Documents/Multikulturalismus%20in%20Kanada%20-%20Modell%20für%20Deutschland%3F%20%7C%20bpb.webarchive, cited 2014-10-15
”Universitet & högskolor – Högskoleverkets årsrapport 2011, Rapport 2011:8 R”, *Högskoleverket*, tillgänglig på: http://www.hsv.se/download/18.27d86368130216405a680002479/1108R-universitet-hogskolor-arsrapport-2011.pdf, citerad 2012-07-15
”Vänsterpartiet mångfald”, tillgänglig på: http://www.google.com/search?client=safari&rls=en&q=vänsterpartiet+mångfald&ie=UTF-8&oe=UTF-8, citerad 2012-07-15
Xenofilia, förlag & produktionsbolag, tillgänglig på http://www.xenofilia.se/, citerad 2013-01-16
Žižek, Sjavoj, Plenary Speech at ”Walls”, Conference at Birkbeck College, i *Dark matter in the ruins of Imperial culture*, 14–16 September 2007, tillgänglig på: http://www.darkmatter101.org/site/2008/02/19/‘liberal-multiculturalism-is-the-hegemony-—-its-an-empirical-fact’-a-response-to-slavoj-zizek/, citerad 2013-01-09

Interviews

Persson, Anders, Lunds Universitet, Campus Helsingborg, Hus C, Vån. 5, U 306, Helsingborg, 2011-12-14, 14.00–17.00

Sichrovsky, Peter, f.d Generalsekreterare för Österrikiska Frihetspartiet, FPÖ office, Wien, 2002-02-02, 13.00–16.00

Westman, Lasse, Hjorttackegatan 8, Malmö, 2005-12-20, 14.00–16.00

Search → mouse → pointers – click
working background – click browse –
hit whatever you like – open it –
click apply + OK

Printed in Great Britain
by Amazon